Family Celebrations with the

CAKE BOSS™

ALSO BY **BUDDY VALASTRO**

CAKE BOSS: STORIES AND RECIPES FROM MIA FAMIGLIA

BAKING WITH THE CAKE BOSS

COOKING ITALIAN WITH THE CAKE BOSS

Family Celebrations with the CAKE BOSS™

RECIPES FOR GET-TOGETHERS THROUGHOUT THE YEAR

BUDDY VALASTRO

PHOTOGRAPHY BY JOHN KERNICK

BOOK DESIGN BY 3&CO.

ATRIA BOOKS

New York London Toronto Sydney New Delhi

ATRIA BOOKS

A Division of Simon & Schuster, Inc.
1230 Avenue of the Americas
New York, NY 10020

First Atria Books hardcover edition November 2013

ATRIA BOOKS and colophon are trademarks of Simon & Schuster, Inc.

For information about special discounts for bulk purchases, please contact Simon & Schuster Special Sales at
1-866-506-1949 or business@simonandschuster.com.

The Simon & Schuster Speakers Bureau can bring authors to your live event. For more information or to
book an event, contact the Simon & Schuster Speakers Bureau at 1-866-248-3049 or visit our website at
www.simonspeakers.com.

Art Direction and Book Design by Amy Harte and Merideth Harte at 3&Co.
Photography by John Kernick.
Photograph on page 3 by Gloria Belgiovine.

Manufactured in the United States of America

10 9 8 7 6 5 4 3 2 1

Library of Congress Control Number: 2013023936

ISBN 978-1-4516-7433-0
ISBN 978-1-4516-7437-8 (ebook)

THIS IS DEDICATED TO THE ONES I LOVE:

Sofia, Buddy, Marco, and Carlo

Contents

CONTENTS

Introduction

Let me ask you a question: Have you ever had a celebration that didn't involve food?

I haven't. As far as I'm concerned, a party just wouldn't be a party without something to eat and drink, and that's extra-true when it comes to family celebrations. My family, the Valastros, come together around food every day—whether around a table in the lunchroom at the Carlo's Bake Shop factory in Jersey City, spontaneously gathering for dinner at one of our homes scattered among the nearby towns of New Jersey, or getting together on the weekend so the cousins can play together while the adults catch up over a glass (or three) of wine and some antipasti.

Like so many Italian-American families, we have a heightened sense of food and its place in life—to us, certain beloved ingredients and dishes are a connection to our ancestral home of Italy, and also to relatives and friends, many of whom are no longer with us. And so, certain occasions inspire us to go all out, preparing and serving a number of dishes that are traditions in their own right, such as the lamb chops with pistachio crust we serve at Easter or the family's signature stuffing on Thanksgiving or the marinated seafood that we look forward to each Christmas Eve. And it's not just holidays that bring out the nostalgia in us: We also have traditions around birthday parties, tailgate parties, and even things we bake and eat with the kids on bad-weather days every winter.

That's all pretty typical of families that come from similar backgrounds. But when the Valastros get together for a special occasion, there's another dimension to the celebration, one that's uniquely us: These events in our lives are *always* punctuated by a special cake, cupcake, or dessert that captures the essence of the day with an unforgettable visual and—of course—a taste that all in attendance won't soon forget. These desserts are to our celebrations what the halftime show is to the Super Bowl: a spectacle that makes an already special moment extra special.

Sometimes the cakes we make are simple, like the Fourth of July Flag Cake we serve on the nation's birthday, with the stars and stripes made with blueberries and raspberries. Other times, they are over the top, such as the Easter Basket Cake. Sometimes we go for individual items such as the glitzy little cupcakes with top hats we put out or pass on New Year's Day.

In this book, I'm delighted to give you a look inside the Valastro family and how we mark the moments in each year with special food and unforgettable desserts. As always, my fondest wish is that my family's traditions and recipes help inspire good times for yours.

Photograph at right by Gloria Belgiovine

How to Use This Book

This book takes you through a delicious year in the life of the Valastro family, starting with New Year's Day and running right through New Year's Eve.

Along the way, it presents recipes for dishes that can be served at many special occasions including the big holidays such as Valentine's Day, Easter, Memorial Day, the Fourth of July, and Thanksgiving. It also shares my family's favorite go-to crowd-pleasers for birthday parties, cocktail parties, tailgate parties, and other celebrations.

And, of course, at the end of each chapter there is a recipe and decorating instructions for the main event: a theme cake or dessert.

A few notes before we dig in and start cooking and baking.

Use the Recipes as You Like

The recipes in each chapter were gathered together to complement one another—after all, we've been serving many of them together in my family for generations. But that doesn't mean that you have to serve all of them at the same time. In most cases, you should think of what's presented for each occasion as options, rather than a set menu. You can also weave these dishes into your own menus, blending my family's favorites with your own. Most of the dishes can be served at any time of year, or even as everyday lunches or dinners.

Make the Recipes Your Own

The recipes in this book are simple, because I believe that cooking at home should be easy and fun, allowing you to enjoy your time and the company of friends and family. So, when cooking from this book, please don't stress if you don't have the exact ingredients I call for: One type of herb can often be replaced with another, and the same goes for mushrooms, vinegars, and other ingredients. By the same token, if you're a comfortable and confident home cook, by all means improvise a little and bring your own flair to the recipes.

Cake Basics

Although they look dramatically different, most of the theme cakes and cupcakes in this book are made with the same basic cake recipes, fillings, frostings, and decorating tools and techniques—all of that information is included at the back of the book, starting on page 283. I suggest you read the basics there before making any of the individual cake recipes or doing any of the decorating.

NEW YEAR'S DAY BRUNCH

New Year's Day used to be pretty funny at Carlo's Bake Shop: The family business was open, as it was on so many holidays, but the employees, beat from celebrating the night before, were good for nothing, but it didn't matter, because the customers—who'd been doing their own thing on New Year's Eve—mostly stayed home. Finally, in the mid-1990s, we decided to keep the bakery closed on January 1, and I'm glad we did because it's really a day to be with the family and think about the year that just ended, and the one ahead. Ever since Lisa and I married, we have celebrated New Year's Day at her Aunt Enza's house in Sayreville, New Jersey. Most of my mother-in-law Gloria's family attends, and my favorite part of the afternoon is that everybody gets in the kitchen to help out with the cooking, or pitches in by bringing a dish of their own. In the following pages, you'll find some of my favorite recipes for welcoming the New Year.

ASPARAGUS FRITTATA

{ SERVES 6 TO 8 }

Among my mother-in-law Gloria's many specialties is frittatas, which she makes throughout the year, and always serves on New Year's Day. A frittata is an Italian omelet, and it's about a million times easier to make than the French version, which involves folding the cooked egg over the filling, then sliding the whole delicate thing out of the pan without breaking it. In making a frittata, you simply bake the filling right into the eggs; getting it out of the pan couldn't be easier because it's so sturdy. Frittatas are wonderful for entertaining because they can be set out as part of a buffet, and are delicious at room temperature.

2 teaspoons olive oil

1 pound thin asparagus, washed, woody stems removed

Kosher salt

8 large eggs

2 tablespoons half-and-half or milk

Finely grated zest of ½ lemon

Freshly ground black pepper

Fresh flat-leaf parsley (leaves and stems), coarsely chopped, for garnish

1. Position a rack in the center of the oven and preheat to 400°F.

2. Heat a large, nonstick, ovenproof skillet over medium-high heat. Add the olive oil and tip and tilt the pan to coat it, letting the oil heat. Add the asparagus and season with salt. Cook, shaking the pan occasionally to ensure even cooking, until the asparagus is al dente and lightly browned in some places, about 4 minutes.

3. Meanwhile, put the eggs, half-and-half, lemon zest, and a generous pinch of salt and pepper in a medium bowl, and whisk together.

4. Lower the heat to medium. Pour the egg mixture into the skillet. Using tongs or a fork (taking care not to scrape the nonstick surface), arrange the asparagus spears so that none are sticking out over the top of the egg mixture. Cook until the eggs look set around the sides of the pan, about 5 minutes, and the vegetables on the bottom are slightly browned (it's fine if the eggs brown a little as well); if the bottom starts to brown too quickly, lower the heat slightly.

5. Transfer the pan to the oven and cook until eggs are fully set and no longer look runny, 6 to 8 minutes. Remove the pan from the oven and season lightly with salt and pepper, if desired. Let cool a few minutes in the pan, then transfer to a large serving platter by sliding it out of the pan, keeping the upward-facing side up. Garnish with parsley, if desired, slice into 6 or 8 portions and serve.

ORZO WITH HAM, PEAS, & GOAT CHEESE

{ SERVES 4 TO 6 }

I've been eating pasta with ham, peas, and Parmesan all my life. The combination works because the fresh, green flavor of the peas is a perfect contrast to the salty ham and cheese. I'm used to enjoying those flavors with orecchiette (ear-shaped pasta) or mezze (half) rigatoni. But one day, left alone in the house to fend for myself, I whipped up this version with on-hand ingredients such as orzo and goat cheese, which melts into a quick sauce, coating the pasta and other ingredients. Now it's a dish we have in our repertoire, serving it at home, and bringing it to family get-togethers like the one we throw on New Year's Day.

Kosher salt
1¼ cups dried orzo
1 cup defrosted frozen peas (see note)
4 ounces soft fresh goat cheese, crumbled
3 tablespoons extra-virgin olive oil
Freshly squeezed juice of 1 large lemon (3 to
    4 tablespoons)
⅓ pound country ham (about ⅔ cup),
    trimmed of excess fat, sliced about
    ¼-inch thick
⅓ cup (loosely packed) fresh mint, chopped

1. Bring a large pot of salted water to a boil. Add the orzo and cook until it is al dente, about 8 minutes. Meanwhile, place the peas in a colander and set it in the sink.

2. When the orzo is done cooking, use a Pyrex measuring cup or other heatproof vessel to scoop out and reserve about ¼ cup of the cooking liquid, then drain the orzo in the colander over the peas (this will quickly cook the peas).

3. Immediately transfer the pasta and peas to a heatproof mixing bowl. Add the goat cheese and stir, gently mashing the cheese with a wooden spoon to help it incorporate into the hot orzo. Add the olive oil, lemon juice, and some of the reserved pasta water to help the cheese emulsify to a saucelike consistency (start with 1 tablespoon and add more as needed). Stir in the ham and the mint.

4. Transfer the pasta to a serving bowl; serve warm.

Frozen Peas: *I don't usually use frozen vegetables, but frozen peas are an exception: when fresh peas are picked, their sugar turns into starch almost right away. Frozen peas, on the other hand, still have all that sweetness locked in, so they are usually a better choice. On top of that, it's a real pain to remove fresh peas from the pod, so I use frozen peas all year long.*

ANTIPASTO SALAD

{ SERVES 4 TO 6 }

Two of the iconic New Jersey catering halls of my youth were the Park Casino and Macaluso's. In fact, to this day, we still celebrate family milestones, such as my daughter Sofia's First Communion, at Macaluso's. A version of this salad has been a part of the cocktail hour at both of those venues since I was a little kid: It's a can't-miss proposition that brings together a bunch of the most popular flavors and ingredients from the Italian-American pantry: olives, marinated mushrooms, roasted peppers, mozzarella, and salami. It's a very versatile recipe: You can leave out the ingredients you don't like, or replace them with other antipasti staples, such as jarred, marinated artichokes.

In addition to being perfect for an open house, this salad makes a quick and easy lunch that can be pulled together at the last second from on-hand ingredients.

1 tablespoon plus 2 teaspoons
  balsamic vinegar
3 tablespoons extra-virgin olive oil
3 cups (loosely packed) salad greens,
  such as arugula or baby spinach
Kosher salt
Freshly ground black pepper
½ cup jarred marinated mushrooms, drained
6 ounces jarred roasted peppers, drained and
  sliced into bite-sized pieces
½ cup marinated or jarred olives, preferably
  pitted, drained
½ pound fresh mozzarella, thinly sliced
4 ounces dried salami, thinly sliced

1. Put the vinegar in a large mixing bowl. Whisk in the olive oil, a few drops at a time at first, and then in a slow, steady stream until it emulsifies with the vinegar. Add the salad greens to the bowl, season with salt and pepper, and toss gently with tongs to coat.

2. Transfer the salad greens to a serving bowl. Add the mushrooms, peppers, olives, mozzarella, and salami in small piles atop the greens. (Do not toss.) Serve family style.

What's In a Name? *Many people think that "antipasto" means "before the pasta" but it actually means "before the meal."*

PECAN CINNAMON BUNS

{ MAKES 8 }

Shown here with Chocolate Pots de Crème, page 17.

Carlo's Bake Shop doesn't make or sell cinnamon buns. I wish we could, but the only way to enjoy this classic breakfast indulgence is right from the oven when they're warm and gooey, and we don't bake anything to order. The only problem is that my kids all *love* cinnamon buns with their dense pastry and sugary glaze. Once in a while we let them order these decadent concoctions from another bakery or even a chain shop, but on New Year's Day, we bake our own homemade cinnamon buns as a special treat at home before heading out to see the rest of the family. These are easier than they might seem, and produce a sweet, cinnamon aroma that fills the entire house, the perfect way to begin the first morning of the year. Be sure to start these ahead of time, so the dough has time to rise.

FOR THE DOUGH:

¾ cup half-and-half

¼ cup granulated sugar

One packet active dry yeast
   (about 2¼ teaspoons)

1 large egg

½ teaspoon pure vanilla extract

2¾ cups all-purpose flour, plus more
   for rolling

¾ teaspoon kosher salt

¼ cup unsalted butter, plus
   more for greasing the bowl

FOR THE FILLING:

7 tablespoons unsalted butter

½ cup granulated sugar

2 tablespoons ground cinnamon

½ cup pecans, toasted and chopped
   (see note)

FOR THE GLAZE:

½ stick (4 tablespoons) unsalted butter,
   melted

1½ cups confectioners' sugar

¼ cup plus 1 tablespoon half-and-half

Kosher salt

1. To make the dough: Put the half-and-half, ¼ cup water, and 1 tablespoon of the sugar in a small, heavy saucepan and set it over medium heat. Cook until the temperature is slightly above lukewarm to the touch, 1 to 2 minutes.

2. Transfer the mixture to the bowl of a stand mixer and sprinkle the yeast over the top. Agitate the bowl gently to help it incorporate, then let rest, undisturbed, until the mixture appears foamy, about 5 minutes. Whisk in the butter, egg, vanilla extract, and the remaining 3 tablespoons of sugar.

3. Put the flour and salt in a small bowl. Set the stand mixer on low speed with the dough attachment. Add the dry ingredients in 2 batches, stopping to scrape down the sides of the bowl with a rubber spatula as necessary, until a dough begins to form, 2 to 3 minutes. If the dough is sticking to the sides of the bowl, add an additional tablespoon of flour to help it form a smooth ball.

4. Lightly grease a mixing bowl with butter. Transfer the dough to the bowl. Cover tightly with plastic wrap and a towel, and set in a warm place to rise until the dough is doubled in size, about 1 hour 20 minutes.

5. To make the filling: Melt the 7 tablespoons butter in a small, heavy saucepan set over low heat. Use 1 tablespoon to grease a 9-by-13-inch by 2 inches (high) glass baking dish. Put the sugar, cinnamon, pecans, and 2 tablespoons of the melted butter in a medium mixing bowl. Stir together with a fork.

6. Roll out the dough onto a lightly floured work surface and, using a rolling pin, roll into a 12-by-18 inch rectangle with a long side facing you. Brush the dough with the remaining 5 tablespoons melted butter, leaving a ½-inch border on the long end farthest from you. Sprinkle the cinnamon-sugar mixture evenly over the dough, leaving the far border uncovered. Wet the border lightly with water. Then, starting with the end of the dough closest to you, roll the dough tightly around the filling. Continue rolling the dough away from you (like you would roll a carpet), pressing lightly on the dough to help seal the end. Trim away 1 inch of dough from each end of the roll, then slice the remaining dough into 8 equal (2-inch-long) buns.

7. Transfer the buns to the prepared baking dish. Cover tightly with plastic wrap and towels and let rise in a warm spot until doubled again in thickness, about 2½ hours (alternatively, you can let this rise overnight in the refrigerator; remove it one hour before baking). Preheat the oven to 325°F and set a rack in the center of the oven. Bake until the buns are lightly golden on the outside and no longer gooey in the center, about 35 minutes. Remove and let cool slightly, about 10 minutes.

8. Meanwhile, make the glaze: Melt 4 more tablespoons butter in a small saucepan. In a mixing bowl, whisk together the confectioners' sugar, ¼ cup half-and-half (you can use water or milk here, too), and a pinch of salt. Whisk in the melted butter. Drizzle each of the rolls with some of the confectioners' sugar glaze. Serve warm.

Toasting and Chopping Nuts:

Toasting nuts before using them in baking, or in any kind of cooking, really, is a great way to unlock their flavor. Put the nuts in a dry pan and set the pan over medium heat. Toast the nuts, shaking the pan constantly to keep them from scorching, and continue to toast them until they are fragrant, 2 to 3 minutes. Transfer the nuts to a bowl to cool. If the nuts need to be chopped, pulse them a few times in a food processor fitted with the steel blade, or put them on your cutting board and crush them lightly with the bottom of a clean, heavy pan, then chop them with a chef's knife.

CHOCOLATE POTS DE CRÈME

{ SERVES 8 }
Photograph on page 14.

If there will be chocoholics present at your New Year's Day celebration, make this dessert! These decadent little potted cooked creams are rich and luscious and ridiculously easy to make. To really drive the chocolate flavor home, top each serving with a light dusting of cocoa powder or a shower of chocolate shavings.

2 pints heavy cream
1 vanilla bean, split down the center, seeds
    scraped and reserved, pod discarded
½ teaspoon instant espresso powder
¼ cup granulated sugar
⅛ teaspoon kosher salt
3 ounces semisweet chocolate,
    coarsely chopped
3 ounces bittersweet chocolate,
    coarsely chopped
8 large egg yolks

1. Position a rack in the center of the oven and preheat the oven to 350°F.

2. Put 2¾ cups of the heavy cream, the vanilla seeds, instant espresso powder, sugar, and salt in a small, heavy saucepan and bring to a boil over medium heat. Turn off the heat and add the chocolate, stirring until melted, returning the pot to the stovetop over medium heat for a few seconds, if needed, to fully melt it.

3. Beat the eggs in a large bowl. Starting with a small amount (to avoid scrambling the eggs), slowly whisk the chocolate mixture into the egg mixture.

4. Evenly fill eight 6-ounce ramekins or custard cups with some of chocolate mixture; place them in a roasting pan and fill the pan with warm water until it reaches three-quarters up the side of the ramekins. Carefully transfer to the oven. Bake until the sides of the *pots de crème* are set and the centers are only slightly jiggly, 20 to 25 minutes. Remove from the oven and carefully take the cups out of the water bath using oven mitts or tongs. Let cool slightly, or chill if making ahead (can be served warm or chilled).

5. Whip the remaining 1⅓ cups cream and serve the *pots* dolloped with whipped cream.

STRAWBERRY NAPOLEONS

{ SERVES 4 }

Classic, custard-filled napoleons with black and white icing have been a regular offering at Carlo's Bake Shop for generations, but when it comes to a special occasion like New Year's Day, we like to change it up at home with a colorful strawberry variation. This is a vibrant, celebratory dessert, perfect for ringing in the New Year. We use our own homemade dough, but to make this recipe as foolproof as possible, it calls for store-bought puff pastry.

1 sheet frozen puff pastry, thawed
2 cups heavy cream
2 tablespoons seedless strawberry jam
1 quart fresh strawberries, washed, stemmed, and thinly sliced
Confectioners' sugar, for dusting

1. Position a rack in the center of the oven and preheat to 350°F.

2. Unfold the puff pastry onto a clean work surface and cut into 12 equal rectangles. Transfer to a parchment-paper–lined baking sheet and bake until golden and puffed, 13 to 15 minutes. Remove the sheet from the oven and let the puff pastry cool completely.

3. Meanwhile, whip the cream until stiff peaks form. Then, using a spatula, fold the jam into the whipped cream until incorporated.

4. To assemble the napoleons, lay out four pieces of puff pastry. Top each with a thin layer of strawberry slices, then add a generous dollop of whipped cream; spread slightly to coat the strawberries. Dust with confectioners' sugar. Repeat the layering once, then top each stack with a final third piece of puff pastry. Dust once more with confectioners' sugar and serve.

NEW YEAR'S DAY
TOP HAT CUPCAKES

{ MAKES 24 CUPCAKES }

These elegant little cupcakes are the perfect way to usher in the New Year, with a fondant top hat and glittery crystal sugar that capture the energy of the occasion. They actually look much more difficult to produce than they are because the top hats are a breeze to make: You just punch out two different sized pieces of fondant and attach them with the help of a little water. Some variety of black and white frosting and cake is the way to go here, to reflect the formality of the occasion.

These are ideal for a New Year's Day buffet because they are single-serving portions, but you can also make them for New Year's Eve instead of the New Year's Eve Cake on page 279, and vice versa.

1 pound black fondant
6 cups white Decorator's Buttercream (page 302)
   in a bag fitted with #6 star tip
About ⅓ cup gold crystal sugar
About ⅓ cup silver crystal sugar
About ⅓ cup candy dragées
24 cupcakes, make with Vanilla Cake (page 292), Chocolate Cake (page 294), or other cake of your choosing

TOOLS & EQUIPMENT
Water pen
1¼-inch and 1½-inch and round punches

a

b

d

e

1. To make the top hats, roll about half of the fondant out to a sheet, ⅛-inch thick. Use the 1½-inch punch (a) to punch out 24 circles and set aside. Roll the other half of the fondant into a 1-inch-thick sheet. Use the 1¼-inch punch to punch out 24 circles.

2. Use a water pen (b) to fix the narrower, taller pieces in the center of the wider, thinner pieces to make 24 top hats (c).

3. Using the buttercream bag, pipe a swirl of buttercream about 1½ inches high on top of each cupcake (d).

4. Sprinkle a little gold sugar on top of each cake, then a little silver (e), then a few dragées. (See tip.)

5. Set a top hat on top of the icing on each cupcake (f).

Tip: *When working with the crystal sugar and dragées, have each in its own bowl and work over the bowl so that any extra falls into the bowl and doesn't go to waste.*

f

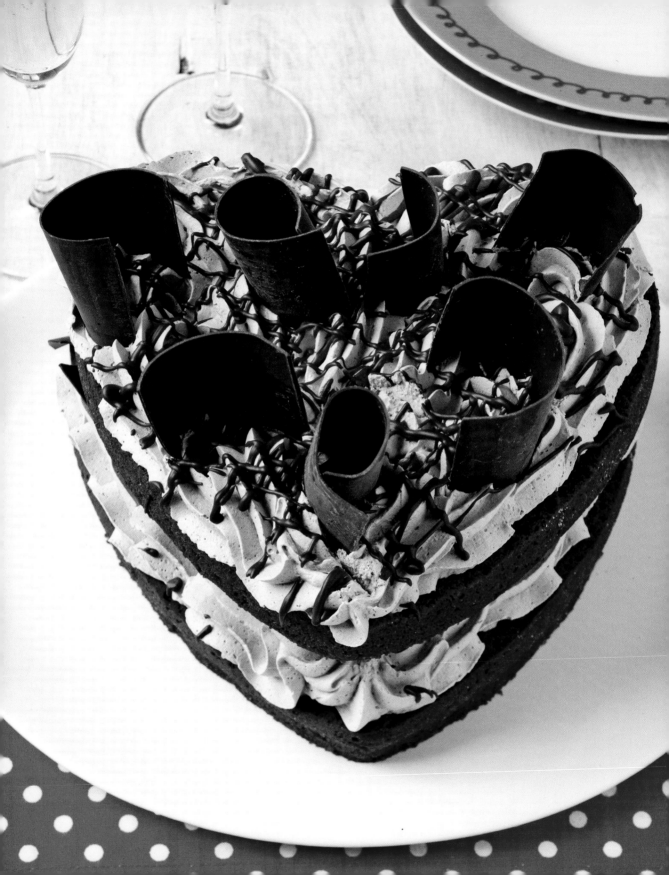

VALENTINE'S DAY DINNER FOR TWO

The recipes in this chapter are extra special to me because Lisa and I don't celebrate Valentine's Day the way we used to. In years past, we sent the kids to relatives' homes and Lisa cooked me a feast of lobster (or, sometimes, king crab), risotto, and creamed spinach, and then I'd make dessert, or desserts, with a chocolate semi-freddo and a version of the heart-shaped cake we've been selling at Carlo's Bake Shop for generations. It was a special, candle-lit evening for two, and some of the most treasured time we've ever spent together. So, if it was so special, why don't we celebrate the way we used to? Because our fourth child, Carlo, was born on February 14, so that's his day now. We wouldn't have it any other way, although I do still make Lisa the heart cake, and we enjoy it together late at night, after the rest of the family has gone to bed.

Note: *The desserts in this chapter are scaled to serve more than two people to make it easy for you to use them for any occasion you like, or perhaps for a Valentine's Day dinner party. The savory recipes can also be multiplied easily.*

SMOKED SALMON RISOTTO

{ SERVES 2 TO 4 }

When I eat seafood, such as lobster, for a main course, I like to double down and complement it with another seafood dish, such as this risotto. It's an unusual risotto in which smoked salmon and soft, tart cheese are combined, as they would be in a tea sandwich or on a bagel. This is another dish inspired by memories of my favorite catering halls—it was a specialty of the Park Casino and its owner, Joe, a dear friend of my father and my family.

To make this especially creamy, stir in two egg yolks at the end; just be sure to do it off the heat to keep them from scrambling.

4 tablespoons unsalted butter

1 tablespoon olive oil

1 shallot, finely chopped

Kosher salt

1½ cups risotto rice, such as arborio rice
  (see note)

½ cup dry white wine

5 cups seafood stock or chicken stock,
  simmering on a back burner

¼ cup half-and-half

½ cup fresh goat cheese, or
  Philadelphia Cream Cheese

2 egg yolks

½ pound smoked salmon, diced

Lemon wedges

Black pepper

Fresh dill

1. Heat 2 tablespoons of the butter and the oil in a Dutch oven or heavy-bottomed saucepan. Add the shallot and season with a pinch of salt. Cook, stirring occasionally, until softened but not browned, about 2 minutes. Add the rice and cook, stirring, to coat it with the fat, 1 to 2 minutes. Pour in the white wine (it should hiss on contact) and, cook, stirring, until just absorbed.

2. Start adding the simmering stock slowly, ladling in ½ cup at a time, and stirring constantly until it is almost completely absorbed by the rice. Continue adding the liquid in batches until it is almost fully absorbed, about 15 minutes, then add it in small increments until the risotto is al dente and creamy.

3. Remove the Dutch oven from the heat and stir in the remaining 2 tablespoons butter, the half-and-half, cheese and egg yolks. Fold in the salmon, and season with salt. Finish by stirring in a squeeze of lemon, the black pepper, and dill. Serve.

The Rice Stuff: *Don't torture yourself when selecting the rice for risotto—the three main types are arborio, vialone nano, and carnaroli. Although some believe certain types are better for certain kinds of risotto, I find that they all work well. Use whatever's convenient and put your time and energy into cooking the actual dish.*

WHOLE STEAMED LOBSTERS WITH GARLIC BUTTER

{ SERVES 2 }

Lobster is, hands down, one of my favorite special occasion foods. Fortunately, Lisa loves it, too. Along with king crab claws, this is our favorite dish from the sea and we always eat one or the other (or both) on Valentine's Day. For me, the only way to dress lobster is with hot, melted garlic butter, dipping the succulent meat into it.

1 tablespoon whole black peppercorns
2 dried bay leaves
2 live lobsters, about 1½ pounds each
1 clove garlic, finely chopped
¼ pound (1 stick) unsalted butter
Pinch kosher salt

1. Pour 1 to 2 inches cold water into the bottom of a large stockpot or lobster pot. Add the black peppercorns and bay leaves. If you have a rack or steamer basket to fit the pot, set it inside. Bring the water to a boil over high heat. Quickly add the lobsters, head-first, and immediately cover the pot tightly. Bring the water back to a boil and let steam until the shells are bright red and the meat is just cooked through, about 10 minutes.

2. Meanwhile, put the garlic and butter in a small, heavy saucepan set over medium heat. When the butter is fully melted, tilt the pan to collect the butter to one side, and use a spoon to skim off and discard any white particles that have floated to the top. Season the butter with a pinch of salt.

3. When the lobsters are done, remove them from their pot using tongs and let them drain briefly in a colander. Pat dry with paper towels and serve warm with the garlic butter in a wide, shallow bowl for dipping.

Seeing Red: *When cooking lobster, as far as I'm concerned, there's only one foolproof way to know that it's done: when its claws turn bright, bright red.*

CREAMED SPINACH

{ SERVES 2 TO 4 AS A SIDE DISH }

Most people think of creamed spinach as a side dish for beef, because you usually see it served in steakhouses. But, my father, who was a very open-minded and creative home cook, used to serve creamed spinach with seafood and it didn't take long for me to see how well the two get along. The creamy, garlicky green makes a wonderful complement to lobster here, and is also delicious alongside everything from white fish such as halibut to tuna and swordfish.

For an extra hit of flavor and/or texture, stir a little grated Parmesan into the spinach and/or top it with toasted breadcrumbs.

2 boxes frozen spinach, 10 ounces each
1½ tablespoons unsalted butter
3 tablespoons finely chopped shallot
1 small clove garlic, finely chopped
Kosher salt
½ teaspoon all-purpose flour
1¼ cups heavy cream

1. Bring a medium pot of water to a boil, add the spinach, and cook just until thawed. Drain in a colander and, when cool enough to handle, squeeze the spinach dry in batches, using your hands to extract as much water as possible.

2. Heat a large skillet over medium high heat, then add the butter and heat until it melts and turns foamy. Add the shallots and garlic and cook, stirring with a wooden spoon, until softened but not browned, about 3 minutes. Season with salt and whisk in the flour, then the cream. Add the spinach and toss or stir well to coat.

3. Serve the spinach warm from a serving bowl or alongside fish or meats.

CHOCOLATE SEMIFREDDO WITH RASPBERRY SAUCE

(SERVES 6 }

Photograph on page 32.

I had my first semifreddo a few years ago when my family traveled to Rome to visit our ancestral home. During that trip, Lisa and I stole away for a private lunch. Even though we may not be fully fluent in Italian, we had a great time communicating with the owner, a kindly old man who I felt an instant kinship with: I had an instinct that he had learned the business from his old man and had been working in the place since he was a kid. At the end of the meal, he didn't even show us dessert menus, but rather brought us two semifreddos. The name means semi-frozen, and it's a classic dessert in Italy. This is my version, with sauce made with one of Lisa's favorite ingredients, raspberries.

Vegetable oil or cooking spray

5 ounces bittersweet chocolate bars, coarsely chopped

½ teaspoon pure vanilla extract

Kosher salt

2 large egg whites

1 cup granulated sugar

1 cup heavy cream

One 10-ounce bag frozen raspberries, thawed

1. Grease an 8-inch loaf pan and line it with a large piece of plastic wrap or parchment paper, letting it hang over by 3 inches on all sides. Place the chocolate in a heatproof bowl and set it over a pot of simmering water, or put it in a double boiler over simmering water, not letting the bowl touch the water. Cook, stirring frequently, until melted. Stir in the vanilla and a scant pinch of salt; set the bowl aside.

2. Place a clean, heatproof bowl over the simmering water, or set a double boiler over simmering water, and whisk the egg whites and ½ cup of the sugar in the bowl to blend, moving the bowl on and off the heat as necessary to keep the whites from cooking. Beat the egg white mixture with an electric mixer at medium-high speed until stiff peaks form, about 10 minutes.

3. Wipe the mixer's blades clean with a paper towel or kitchen towel. In a separate bowl off the stove, beat the heavy cream until soft peaks form, about 3 minutes.

4. Fold the melted chocolate into the egg white mixture until blended, then gently fold in the whipped cream. Pour the mixture into the prepared pan, smoothing the top with a spatula. Cover gently with the ends of the plastic wrap and freeze at least 8 hours.

5. Meanwhile, make the sauce. Set aside about ⅓ cup raspberries. Put the remaining raspberries and the remaining ½ cup of sugar in the bowl of a food processor fitted with the steel blade and process until smooth. Strain through a fine sieve, pressing down with the bottom of a ladle to extract as much liquid as possible. Discard the solids and set the sauce aside. (The sauce can be made up to 2 days ahead and stored in an airtight container in the refrigerator.)

6. Remove the semifreddo from the freezer and let thaw a few minutes to help it release from the pan; turn out onto a platter and remove the plastic wrap. (If the semifreddo is difficult to turn out, dip the bottom of the loaf pan in warm water to help loosen it.) Slice the semifreddo into 6 slices and put each slice on a plate. Top with raspberry sauce and reserved raspberries.

GRAND MARNIER SOUFFLÉS

{ MAKES 6 }

Beyond a dramatic theme cake, there might be no dessert more special than a soufflé, and there's something especially elegant about one flavored with Grand Marnier, an orange liqueur. I make these for Lisa once in a while as a romantic surprise, and I recommend them to you for Valentine's Day or any special occasion.

¼ cup unsalted butter, plus more for greasing
½ cup granulated sugar, plus more
    for dusting
3 tablespoons all-purpose flour
⅔ cup whole milk
¼ teaspoon kosher salt
¼ teaspoon finely grated orange zest
5 eggs, yolks and whites separated
2 tablespoons Grand Marnier or
    other orange liqueur
Confectioners' sugar, for dusting

1. Position a rack in the center of the oven and preheat to 400°F.

2. Generously butter the bottom and sides of six 4-ounce ramekins. Coat them entirely with granulated sugar, knocking out any excess.

3. In a medium, heavy saucepan, melt the butter over medium heat. Add the flour and cook, stirring with a wooden spoon or heatproof spatula, until the butter and flour come together in a thick, light beige mixture (a roux). Cook, stirring frequently, another 1 to 2 minutes. Slowly pour in the milk, stirring constantly. Stir in the salt and orange zest, and bring the mixture to a simmer; continue to cook, stirring occasionally, until thickened, about 3 minutes. Remove the saucepan from the heat and let cool slightly, about 10 minutes.

4. Meanwhile, in a large bowl, beat the egg yolks. Stir in the warm milk mixture, then the Grand Marnier.

5. In the clean, dry bowl of a stand mixer fitted with the whisk attachment, beat the egg whites on high speed until soft peaks form. With the motor still running, pour in the ½ cup sugar very slowly, one or two tablespoons at a time. Keep beating until all of the sugar is incorporated and the egg whites are just shy of holding stiff peaks. Working in two batches, gently fold the whites into the egg–milk mixture, using a spatula, until no streaks remain.

6. Spoon the soufflé mixture into the prepared ramekins, and smooth the tops. Set the ramekins in a roasting pan. Fill the pan with about ½ inch of hot water. Bake the soufflés, without opening the oven, until puffed and golden on the outside and slightly jiggly in the center, 18 to 20 minutes. Remove, transfer the ramekins to plates and dust with confectioners' sugar. Serve immediately.

a

b

c

d

VALENTINE'S DAY HEART CAKE

{ MAKES ONE HEART-SHAPED CAKE }

You gotta step up at Valentine's Day, and this cake makes it easy to do that for your sweetheart, even if you aren't an experienced cake decorator: It doesn't call for any special tools or equipment, except for a piping bag and a parchment pencil (see box), and the cake is baked in a heart-shaped form, so you're already ahead of the game when you start decorating. I like making this cake with Red Velvet Cake (page 298), which is perfect for the heart theme. You can really go to town and adapt this cake in all kinds of ways: Change it up by using white chocolate instead of dark (or a combination), or vary the fillings by using chocolate chips or a chopped up chocolate bar (even a simple Hershey's Milk Chocolate bar would be awesome) in the center, or add cereal, like crushed Cocoa Pebbles to the center to add texture. (The only thing you want to avoid is anything too fudgy or thick, which won't get along with the chocolate mousse.)

You can also top this cake with red fruit, such as strawberries or pitted cherries.

ONE HEART-SHAPED CAKE

One 9-inch cake of your choosing (pages 292 to 298)
My Dad's Chocolate Mousse (page 308), in a piping bag fit with #6 star tip
Chocolate Ganache (page 309), at room temperature (just warm enough to be pourable)
2 to 3 ounces store-bought chocolate shavings, dark or light chocolate

TOOLS & EQUIPMENT

10- to-12-inch cardboard circle, preferably gold
Parchment paper

1. Prepare the Cake (page 284): Use a serrated knife to trim the crusty top off the cake, and cut the cake in half horizontally (a) . Pipe a dab of mousse into the center of the board and set the bottom of the cake on top of it. (The mousse will hold it in place.)

2. Fill the Cake: Top the cake bottom with mousse by first piping the mousse around the perimeter in a swirl pattern (b), then filling in the center. (Make the perimeter as uniform and attractive as possible; this cake will not be iced or covered with fondant, so the icing will show from the sides.)

3. Pour the ganache over the mousse (c); use as little or as much as you like based on your appetite for decadence. Spread the ganache over the mousse gently with a cake spatula.

4. Embed some of the chocolate shavings into the mousse on the bottom layer (d). Set the top of the cake on top of the mousse.

5. Finish the Cake: Pipe with icing following the instructions above. Use a parchment pencil (see below) to drizzle ganache over the cake (e), first drizzling it from left to right, and then from top to bottom.

6. Top the cake with chocolate shavings, sticking them into the ganache so they stand up (f).

PARCHMENT PENCIL

For a more elegant application of the ganache, use a parchment pencil.

Making a parchment pencil: It's quick and easy to make a parchment pencil for small jobs such as writing on cakes, drizzling molten chocolate, or piping small design elements. Parchment pencils are also handy for those times when you don't have a pastry bag on hand, or if all of your bags are filled.

To make a parchment pencil: Make a parchment triangle: Cut a 12-inch-square piece of parchment paper diagonally in half, either with scissors, or by laying it on a cutting board or work station and slicing through it with the tip of a very sharp knife, to create two triangles. You will only use one triangle; save the other for the next time.

Make a parchment cone: With one hand, hold the triangle in front of you with the point facing down. Use your other hand to wrap the paper around itself into a cone, coming around twice to use up all the paper.

Tighten the cone: Pinch the wide, open end of the cone with your thumb and forefinger and rub your fingers together repeatedly to tighten the cone. It should still be wide at the open end, in a firm, conical shape.

Fill the cone: Use a tablespoon or small rubber spatula to fill the cone about two-thirds full with the filling of your choice. Hold the cone securely so it doesn't unravel.

Close the top: Roll the top closed over the filling, pressing down to pack the cream in tightly all the way to the bottom.

Cut the bottom: Use scissors to snip off the bottom of the cone. For a plain tip, cut as far up as you need to for the width you desire. For a leaf tip, flatten out the bottom by pressing on it and cut out a "V" shape.

f

BAD WEATHER
BAKING DAY
WITH KIDS

As a businessman, snow days kill me, because they make people want to stay home, rather than brave the elements to visit our bakery, especially if it means waiting in line, as it often does these days. But I believe that there's always a silver lining, even when the weather is truly awful . . . make that *especially* when the weather is truly awful: On snow days when the schools are forced to close, on those weekends when nonstop rainstorms trap us inside, we set up for a full day of cooking and baking with the kids. Even though my family runs a bakery, there's something special about all of us getting together at home and cooking up a storm: We make sandwiches and soup, cookies, and—of course—a cake. There's nothing like cooking together as a family, and these recipes have turned even the coldest, wettest days into an opportunity for having fun and creating memories.

EASY TOMATO SOUP

{ SERVES 4 TO 6 }

Shown with Grilled Cheese Sandwiches with Bacon & Sprouts, recipe on page 44.

Like so many Italian-American families, we canned tomatoes at the end of each summer when I was a kid. (These days, we get together with Lisa's family and turn the tradition into a huge production at the factory.) One of my favorite ways that my mother used them was in a quick and easy tomato soup, finishing it with basil. I especially loved this soup on rainy days. I'd come in from the damp outdoors, take off my shoes, and sit down with my sisters to enjoy it.

My father kept a backyard garden, and there was always basil. When my mother made this soup, she would tell me to go outside and pick some; I still remember its fragrant, summery smell. These days, my son Buddy Jr. keeps his own garden, and if we're cooking something that calls for herbs, we ask him to pick them, the way I used to.

This is a flexible soup that can be as thick or thin as you like.

2 tablespoons unsalted butter

1 large yellow onion, finely chopped

2 cloves garlic, finely chopped

2 cans whole peeled tomatoes, 28 ounces each, crushed by hand with their juice

1 cup chicken stock, plus more if needed

½ cup (loosely packed) fresh basil leaves, washed and coarsely sliced or torn by hand

½ cup heavy cream, half-and-half, or milk

Kosher salt

Freshly ground black pepper

1. Heat a large, heavy pot over medium heat. Add the butter and cook until it is melted and foamy. Add the onion and garlic and cook, stirring occasionally, until softened but not browned, about 4 minutes. Pour in the tomatoes and their juices, then stir in the stock. Raise the heat to high, bring to a boil, then lower the heat so the liquid is simmering. Continue to simmer, stirring occasionally, until the tomatoes begin to break down, about 10 minutes. Set aside 2 tablespoons of the basil, and stir the rest into the pot.

2. Using an immersion blender, or working in batches in a standing blender (see note), puree the soup until almost smooth. Stir in the cream, season with salt and pepper, and adjust the consistency with more cream or chicken stock. Ladle into bowls, and garnish with the remaining basil.

Hot Stuff: *Be careful when blending hot liquids in a standing blender because the contained steam and heat can cause the lid to pop off; a good way to prevent this is to remove the center piece from the blender and cover the hole with a folded, slightly damp kitchen towel. This will allow steam to escape as you work; just don't fill the blender so high that the soup splashes out!*

GRILLED CHEESE SANDWICHES WITH BACON & SPROUTS

{ MAKES 4 SANDWICHES }
Photograph on page 42.

My wife, Lisa, is always trying to find clever ways to get the kids to eat more healthfully, which isn't easy when your family runs a bakery! Her personal philosophy is that, even when a meal isn't necessarily a low-fat or low-calorie affair, you can still teach children to love healthy choices. These grilled cheese sandwiches are a perfect illustration of her approach: The bread is whole wheat or multigrain, there are sprouts in the sandwich, and the sandwiches are cooked in a nonstick pan so very little butter (or mayonnaise) is required.

Not only do these taste great, but they are the ultimate accompaniment to the tomato soup on page 43. Dipping the sandwiches into that soup will chase away the blues on even the nastiest day of the year.

8 slices bacon
8 slices whole wheat or multigrain bread
2 tablespoons butter, at room temperature,
    or mayonnaise
8 slices (about 8 ounces) white
    American cheese
¼ cup alfalfa sprouts

1. Heat a large, heavy skillet over medium heat. Lay the bacon slices side by side (slightly overlapping or wrinkled is fine). Cook, turning and flipping occasionally with tongs, until browned and crispy, 8 to 10 minutes. Remove and drain on a paper-towel–lined plate.

2. Spread one side of each of the bread slices with some of the butter or mayonnaise (about ¾ teaspoon each). Top the unbuttered side of one slice with a piece of cheese, then some of the sprouts and 2 slices of bacon. Top with a second piece of cheese, then a second bread slice, buttered-side up. Repeat with the remaining ingredients.

3. Preheat a griddle or nonstick pan over medium heat. Transfer the sandwiches to the pan and cook, pressing down occasionally on the top of the sandwich, until golden brown and crispy, 2 to 3 minutes. Flip carefully, using a wide spatula, and cook until golden brown and the cheese is melted, about 3 minutes more. (Lower the heat and cover the pan if the bread browns before the cheese is melted.) Cut in half diagonally and serve immediately.

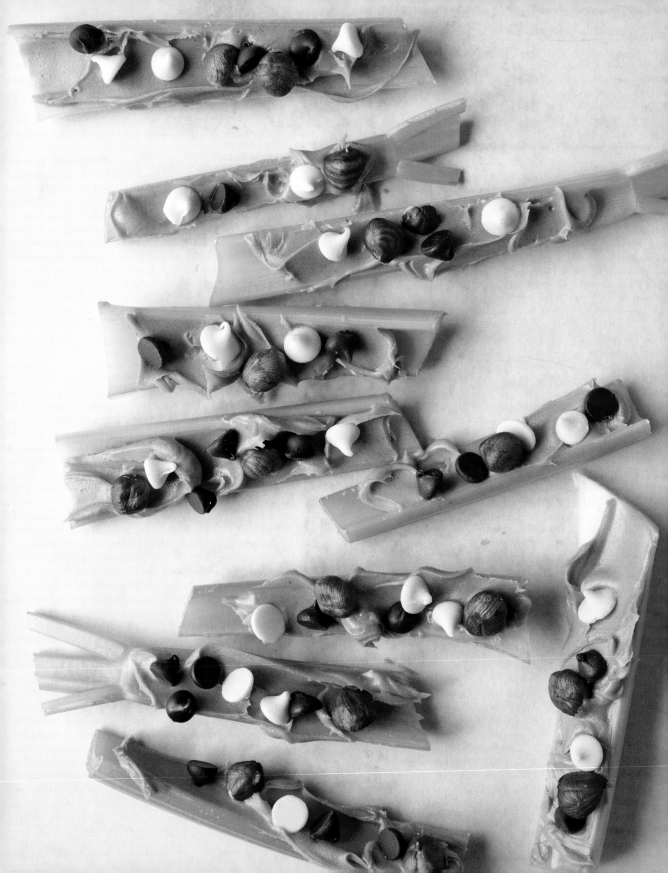

NUTTY BUMPS ON A LOG

{ SERVES 4 }

I don't know who first invented this snack, but it's a brilliant way to get kids to eat celery, by filling the vegetable with peanut butter and decorating it with chocolate chips and hazelnuts. It may not be as impressive as the theme cakes we make at the bakery, but children love filling, decorating, then eating these.

4 large stalks celery, washed, trimmed, and cut in half
$^2/_3$ cup creamy or chunky peanut butter
2 tablespoons white chocolate chips
2 tablespoons semisweet chocolate chips
¼ cup hazelnuts

Using a butter knife, fill each of the celery stalk halves with some of the peanut butter. Decorate by alternating pressing in white chocolate chips, chocolate chips, and hazelnuts down the center of the peanut butter.

APPLE-OATMEAL COOKIES

{ MAKES 1 DOZEN LARGE COOKIES }

My family went through an oatmeal phase one brutal winter when we all wanted a nice hot bowl of oatmeal for breakfast every day. Except for Buddy Jr., who hated oatmeal. Lisa tried everything, but nothing worked, till she tried Granny Smith apples, with a little help from brown sugar and cinnamon. That combination led to these cookies, which are packed with flavor and texture, and just as welcome on a cold, wet day as those bowls of oatmeal were.

FOR THE COOKIES:

1½ cups plus 2 teaspoons unsalted butter, softened at room temperature

2 small Granny Smith apples, peeled, cored, and cut into ½-inch dice

²/₃ cup plus 1 teaspoon light brown sugar

⅛ teaspoon ground cinnamon

Kosher salt

1 large egg

½ teaspoon pure vanilla extract

¾ cup all-purpose flour

½ teaspoon baking soda

1½ cups oats

GLAZE:

1¼ cup confectioners' sugar

¼ teaspoon pure vanilla extract

1. Position a rack in the center of the oven and preheat the oven to 350°F.

2. Heat a small, heavy saucepan over medium-high heat. Add 2 teaspoons of the butter, and let melt. Add the apple, 1 teaspoon of the brown sugar, the cinnamon, and a scant pinch of salt, and stir well to combine. Cook, stirring occasionally, until the apples are slightly softened, about 3 minutes.

3. In the bowl of a stand mixer, cream the remaining butter and brown sugar on medium-high speed until the mixture appears light and fluffy. Add the egg and vanilla and beat until incorporated.

4. Combine the flour, baking soda, and ¼ teaspoon salt in a separate bowl. With the mixer on low, beat in the dry ingredients, then fold in the apples by hand.

5. Line 2 baking sheets with parchment paper. Scoop out 2 tablespoons of dough at a time and arrange them at least 2 inches apart on the prepared cookie sheet. Bake, rotating the sheets top to bottom halfway through baking, until the cookies appear set, 15 to 17 minutes. Remove and let cool for a few minutes on the sheet, then transfer to a baking rack to cool completely.

6. To make the optional glaze: Put the confectioners' sugar, the vanilla extract, and 1 tablespoon water in a medium mixing bowl and whisk until the mixture is smooth. Drizzle the glaze over the cookies using a spoon.

FLOURLESS COCONUT-CHOCOLATE DROPS

{ MAKES 1 DOZEN }
Shown here with Caramel-Nut Clusters, recipe on page 52.

Chocolate macaroons are a popular two-bite snack at Carlo's Bake Shop. These little drops are an easier, at-home way to enjoy the same flavors and similar texture.

4 ounces semisweet chocolate, coarsely chopped, or chocolate chips

4 large egg whites

2 tablespoons granulated sugar

1/8 teaspoon kosher salt

1/2 teaspoon pure vanilla extract

3 cups sweetened shredded coconut

1. Position a rack in the center of the oven and preheat the oven to 325°F.

2. In a microwave or in a bowl set over a saucepan of simmering water, melt the chocolate, stirring occasionally, until smooth. Let cool slightly.

3. Put the egg whites, sugar, salt, vanilla, and coconut in a large bowl, and stir them together with a wooden spoon. Stir in the melted chocolate until well combined.

4. Line a baking sheet with parchment paper or a silicone mat. Dollop the coconut-chocolate mixture onto the sheet in 2-inch balls (about 1¼ cup of the mixture each) about 2 inches apart. Bake until set, 16 to 18 minutes.

   Remove and let cool completely. The drops may be stored in an airtight container at room temperature for 2 to 3 days.

CARAMEL-NUT CLUSTERS

{ MAKES 12 }

Photograph on page 51.

In the old days, at Carlo's Bake Shop, we used to make a classic Italian nougat called *torrone*, made with almonds, sugar, and cinnamon, that we would chop up and sell by the pound. We don't make it anymore because the younger generations don't know it, but I still miss it, and it inspired this contemporary recipe.

Heaping ½ cup unsalted or lightly salted mixed nuts, such as cashews, almonds, and peanuts

12 soft caramels

2 ounces semisweet chocolate, coarsely chopped, or chocolate chips

1. Position a rack in the center of the oven and preheat the oven to 350°F.

2. Finely chop about 2 tablespoons of the mixed nuts, and set aside. Using the palm of your hand, press on each of the caramels to flatten to about half their usual height.

3. Line the bottoms of 12 cups of a mini muffin tin with mixed nuts. The nuts should be packed into the tin well, but in a single, flat layer. Place one flattened caramel over each nut cluster in the tin. Bake until the caramels are slightly melted and sticking to the nuts, 6 to 7 minutes. If needed, press down on the caramels lightly to help the nuts adhere.

4. Meanwhile, in a microwave or a bowl set over a pan of simmering water, melt the chocolate, stirring occasionally, until smooth. Using a teaspoon, dollop some of the melted chocolate over the top of each caramel, smoothing the chocolate with the back of a spoon so it almost fully coats the caramel. Sprinkle each with some of the chopped nuts.

    Refrigerate the clusters in the baking tin until the chocolate is firm, at least 1 hour. Remove from the tins and serve. (The clusters may be held for up to 1 week.)

SPIKY LAYER CAKE

{ MAKES ONE 9-INCH CAKE }

With four kids of my own, and about a million cousins who come and go all the time, I know a little something about being with kids in the kitchen. The main thing when you let a child take on a baking or decorating project is that you set them up for success, and this crazy and colorful layer cake is just the thing, especially on a gray day when the vibrant colors of the frostings will liven things up.

You don't have to use the exact colors that I do here, but use bright ones to create a tie-dyed effect. You can also use whatever cake you like, but there's so much action in the frosting that vanilla or chocolate cakes are the best.

Two 9-inch cakes of your choosing (pages 292 to 298)

A total of 8 cups (1½ recipes) Decorator's Buttercream (page 302) made into 4 colors, 3½ cups pink, 1½ cups each of yellow, blue, and orange (or colors of your choosing)

TOOLS & EQUIPMENT
10- to-12-inch cardboard circle
Piping bag fitted with #6 plain tip

a

b

c

d

e

f

g

h

i

1. Use a serrated knife to trim the crusty top off the cake (a).

2. Set the cardboard circle on your turntable, set a dab of pink frosting in the center, and set a cake on top (b). (The frosting will hold the cake in place.)

3. Use a cake spatula to top the cake with pink frosting (c) (page 285).

4. Set the other cake on top (d).

5. Use the cake spatula to spread the four different color frostings onto the top and sides of the cake, assigning one color to each quarter of the cake (e).

6. Spread and smooth the colors as you turn the table, but do not overmix; you want the colors to streak but not come together into a single blended color (f).

7. Make the frosting spiky by continuing to turn the turntable and lightly spanking the frosting with the spatula's blade on the sides and top (g, h).

8. Use a rubber spatula to carefully add the frostings to the pastry bag, keeping the colors separate by rotating the bag slightly as you add each color and not pressing them together so they will create stripes when piped.

9. Squeeze and pull blobs of multicolored frosting as you rotate the turntable. (i) With the turntable still, pipe swirly blobs on top of the cake (j).

EASTER SUPPER

Easter is one of those holidays that's a little different for my family, because the bakery has always been open, so large celebrations are rare, though we have tried: You might even have seen the episode of *Cake Boss* when my sister Grace, famous in the family for not knowing her way around the kitchen, botched Easter dinner. These days, my immediate family has an intimate, quiet celebration, with just a handful of family. Even though the size and location of the dinner has changed, we have favorite recipes that we turn to over and over for this very special occasion—in other words, in the case of Easter, the dishes are the tradition for us. No matter who's at the table or how many people are in the next room, these are the dishes that will always mean Easter to me.

CROSTINI WITH RICOTTA & HONEY

{ SERVES 4 TO 8 (MAKES 8 GOOD-SIZED CROSTINI) }
Shown here with Baby Spinach & Marinated Artichoke Salad, recipe on page 62.

When it comes to entertaining at home, crostini might be one of my favorite go-tos: a simple piece of toasted bread to which you add toppings such as sautéed chicken livers, white beans, or whatever else feels right at the time. There's nothing unusual about topping crostini with ricotta cheese, but one Easter, moments before guests came into our house, I spontaneously reached for a jar of honey instead of the usual finishing touch of black pepper, and a new tradition was born. The honey, ricotta, and lemon zest all get along great here.

8 1-inch-thick slices from a baguette,
    cut on a long bias
1 tablespoon plus 2 teaspoons
    extra-virgin olive oil
1 cup full-fat ricotta cheese
½ teaspoon finely grated lemon zest
¼ teaspoon kosher salt plus more to taste
1/8 teaspoon freshly ground black
    pepper plus more to taste
2 teaspoons honey

1. Position a rack in the center of the oven and preheat to 350°F. (You can also use a toaster oven preheated to 350°F.)

2. Drizzle or brush the baguette slices with 2 teaspoons extra-virgin olive oil, then toast until lightly golden and crispy, 8 to 10 minutes.

3. Meanwhile, make the ricotta spread. In a bowl, use a rubber spatula to stir together the ricotta, lemon zest, salt, pepper, and remaining tablespoon olive oil.

4. Spoon about 2 tablespoons of the ricotta mixture onto each baguette slice. Top each with about ¼ teaspoon of honey and finish with salt and pepper. Arrange the crostini on a serving plate or platter and serve.

BABY SPINACH & MARINATED ARTICHOKE SALAD

{ SERVES 4 }
Photograph on page 61.

Visit any Italian specialty shop and, behind the counter, you'll see a variety of antipasti: marinated mushrooms, roasted red peppers, house-cured olives. One of my favorites is Roman-style artichokes, which I could eat on their own. Because she knows how much I love them, once, for my birthday, my sister Madeline brought this salad to a potluck dinner at our house and, by the following Easter, I had added it to our holiday repertoire. It's loaded with flavor, like the tangy mustard vinaigrette and the salty capers, and the spinach really bulks it up into something substantial; in fact, if you add some canned or preserved tuna to it, it could be a light lunch on its own.

3 tablespoons white wine vinegar
½ teaspoon Dijon mustard
¼ teaspoon granulated sugar
Kosher salt
Freshly ground black pepper
¼ cup plus 2 tablespoons extra-virgin olive oil
8 cups baby spinach
4 long-stem marinated artichokes,
    halved lengthwise
Canned or preserved tuna (optional)
2 teaspoons capers (in salt or brine)
Scant ¼ cup fresh Parmesan shavings
    (use a vegetable peeler)

1. Put the vinegar, mustard, sugar, and a pinch each of salt and pepper in a medium mixing bowl and whisk them together. Gradually whisk in the olive oil, adding it a few drops at a time at first, and then in a thin stream, until the dressing is emulsified. When ready to serve, add the spinach leaves to the bowl and toss gently to coat.

2. Divide the baby spinach among four large salad plates. Place two artichoke halves on opposite ends of each plate. If adding tuna, flake out of the can with a fork and distribute evenly over the top. Sprinkle the salads with the capers and top with the Parmesan shavings.

CREAMY BLACK PEPPER POLENTA

{ SERVES 4 }
Photograph on page 64.

My wife, Lisa, makes polenta all the time, which is lucky for the rest of us because she has a natural touch with it. Polenta is cornmeal that's cooked in milk, cream, stock, water, or a combination of any or all of the above. Sometimes I explain it to Americans, especially Southerners, and they say, "Oh, grits." Not quite. When polenta is done right, it's as satisfying as mashed potatoes, complementing whatever meat you serve it with and soaking up the sauce on the plate.

This is one of my favorite variations of polenta, with a combination of stock and milk, and just enough black pepper to make its presence known. You can use coarsely ground pepper to heighten its effect, or leave it out for plain polenta. This is also delicious with braised and roasted meats such as short ribs or osso buco. To elevate a beef stew, serve it over polenta instead of egg noodles.

2 cups milk, or more as needed

2 cups chicken stock, or more as needed (optional)

3 teaspoons kosher salt

1 bay leaf

1 cup instant polenta

1 tablespoon unsalted butter

½ teaspoon freshly ground black pepper

Fill a medium saucepan with the milk, 2 cups chicken stock or water, the kosher salt, and the bay leaf; bring to a boil. Add the cornmeal in a very thin stream, whisking constantly and vigorously, so that no clumps form. Simmer until the polenta is thickened (it should still be slightly runny; add more chicken stock, milk or water as needed to adjust the consistency), about 3 to 4 minutes. Turn down the heat to very low and stir in the butter and black pepper. Serve immediately.

PISTACHIO-CRUSTED LAMB CHOPS

{ SERVES 4 }

Shown here with Creamy Black Pepper Polenta, recipe on page 63.

There's only one thing that Italian-Americans eat for the main course at Easter supper: lamb. Although leg of lamb is often the cut of choice, I find that lamb chops can be more surprising, and they're also a little more elegant if you are hosting a formal, sit-down dinner. This recipe produces something a little different: pistachio-crusted chops, coated with a nut–bread mixture. The mint in the breading is a nod to the tradition of eating lamb with mint jelly, which was the way all the old timers did when I was a kid.

This recipe produces two chops per person; the recipe can be scaled up.

1 clove garlic
½ cup raw shelled unsalted pistachios
¼ cup plain fine dried breadcrumbs
1 teaspoon grated lemon zest,
    plus 2 teaspoons fresh lemon juice
¼ cup extra-virgin olive oil
⅔ cup packed fresh mint leaves
1 full rack of lamb (about 1 ½ pounds),
    bones frenched and excess fat trimmed
    (ask your butcher to do this)
¾ teaspoon kosher salt

1. Position a rack in the top third of the oven and preheat to 400°F.

2. Meanwhile, put the garlic, pistachios, breadcrumbs, and lemon zest in the bowl of a food processor fitted with the steel blade and process until finely chopped, about 30 seconds. Add the lemon juice and olive oil and process again until the mixture begins to become pasty. Add the mint leaves and pulse just until incorporated. (The mixture should feel moist to the touch and hold together when you pinch it between your fingers.)

3. Line a baking sheet with aluminum foil. Season the lamb all over with salt and rub with 2 tablespoons olive oil; set on the foil, bones on top but facing down. Using your hands, press the pistachio mixture over the back of the rack of lamb, spreading it evenly, to adhere (it should just coat the meat, not the bones). Roast until the top of the pistachio coating is slightly browned and the lamb is medium rare, 25 to 30 minutes. (A thermometer inserted into the center of the chops should read 135°F.) Remove and pull the ends of the foil over the lamb to loosely tent; let rest 5 minutes.

4. Divide the lamb into chops by slicing between the bones with a sharp chef's knife. Serve with any fallen pieces of the pistachio crust.

ROASTED MUSHROOMS WITH FRESH PARSLEY

{ SERVES 4 }

This is a dish that my mother made all the time when I was growing up. Today, there's so much attention paid to wild mushrooms, which are pretty expensive. But Mama taught me early that if you know what you're doing in the kitchen, you can make even the most basic ingredients delicious. Here, simple baby bella mushrooms are punched up with garlic, shallot, and parsley. Today, we don't just serve this at Easter, but at celebrations all year long, because mushrooms get along with just about anything, and anybody can make these.

Two 8-ounce packages baby bella
    mushrooms, larger ones sliced in half
    or quartered (see note)
3 tablespoons vegetable or canola oil
¼ teaspoon kosher salt, plus more to taste
Scant ⅛ teaspoon freshly ground
    black pepper
2 cloves garlic, finely chopped
1 tablespoon finely chopped shallot
    (about ½ small shallot)
2½ tablespoons unsalted butter
½ teaspoon Dijon mustard
2 tablespoons chopped fresh flat-leaf parsley

1. Position a rack in the center of the oven and preheat to 425°F.

2. Put the mushrooms in a large, shallow baking dish, and add the oil, salt, pepper, garlic, and shallot. Toss to coat the mushrooms with the other ingredients. Cut the butter into pieces and scatter them atop the mushrooms.

3. Roast the mushrooms, stirring once or twice to ensure even cooking, until dark brown and they've lost some of their juices, 15 to 17 minutes. Use a slotted spoon to transfer them to a serving bowl. Season to taste with more salt, if desired, then stir in the mustard and garnish with the parsley.

Sizing Things Up: *It's always best to trim or shape vegetables and other ingredients so that the pieces are about the same size, which ensures that they cook at the same rate.*

CITRUS–OLIVE OIL CAKE

{ SERVES 8 }

Whenever she joins us for Easter dinner, my mother-in-law, Gloria, brings this incredible olive oil cake. We all go nuts for it because it's so incredibly moist and delicious that it doesn't take more than a scattering of lemon and orange zest to really bring it home. This is a wonderful make-ahead dessert for entertaining, not just for Easter, but any time of year.

Unsalted butter, for greasing the pan

2 cups all-purpose flour, plus more for the pan

3 large eggs

2½ cups granulated sugar

1½ cups milk

1¼ cups fruity extra-virgin olive oil

½ teaspoon pure vanilla extract

¼ teaspoon finely grated lemon zest, plus more for garnish

¼ teaspoon finely grated orange zest, plus more for garnish

1 teaspoon baking powder

¼ teaspoon kosher salt

1¼ cups confectioners' sugar

1 tablespoon plus 1 teaspoon freshly squeezed orange juice

1. Position a rack in the center of the oven and preheat the oven to 350°F.

2. Grease a 10-inch Bundt pan or equivalent cake pan lightly with butter, then dust it lightly with flour, tapping out any excess. Put the eggs and granulated sugar in a large bowl and whisk them together, then whisk in the milk, olive oil, vanilla, lemon zest, and orange zest.

3. In a separate bowl, sift the flour, baking powder, and salt. Working in two or three batches, add the dry ingredients to the wet ones, whisking until smooth and fully blended. Pour the batter into the prepared pan.

4. Bake in the oven until the top is golden brown and a toothpick inserted into the center of the cake comes out clean, about 1 hour and 20 minutes. Let cool partially in the pan. Then turn the cake out onto a drying rack and let cool completely.

5. Meanwhile, make the glaze. Using a fork, stir together the confectioners' sugar and orange juice until smooth but thick. Spoon the glaze atop the cooled cake, letting it run down the sides. Garnish the top of the cake with more finely grated lemon and orange zest.

ITALIAN WHEAT PIE

{ MAKES ONE 10-INCH PIE, SERVING 10 TO 12 }

Wheat pie, or *pastiera di grano,* is an Italian Easter specialty. It's not as popular as it once was because it's unfamiliar to our younger customers, but it was *the* Easter dessert when I was a kid, and I will always love it for the one-of-a-kind texture made by boiling down wheat berries and cooking them with butter and orange blossom water. There's just nothing like it, and I encourage you to make it at least once, and see if it doesn't become a part of your gotta-have-it Easter menu.

1 pound ricotta cheese

1 cup granulated sugar

3 tablespoons orange blossom water

½ teaspoon finely grated lemon zest

½ teaspoon finely grated orange zest

3 extra large eggs

1 pound cooked wheat berries, cooled
(about 3 cups)

1 prepared Pasta Frolla (recipe follows)

1. Position a rack in the center of the oven and preheat the oven to 350°F.

2. Put the ricotta cheese, sugar, orange blossom water, lemon zest, and orange zest in the bowl of a stand mixer fitted with the paddle attachment and paddle at low speed until well blended. (You can also mix in a mixing bowl using a wooden spoon.) Add the eggs one at time, mixing until the mixture is smooth, then fold in the cooked wheat berries until well mixed.

3. Pour the mixture into a pie pan lined with Pasta Frolla. Create a lattice top by arranging three parallel strips at even intervals, then laying three strips over them at a perpendicular angle.

4. Bake until puffed, golden brown, and set, but not hard, in the center, about 1 hour. Remove the pan from the oven and let cool completely before serving.

Zesting Citrus Fruits: *There's nothing like a Microplane zester for finely grating zest from lemons, limes, and oranges. Originally a woodworking tool, this planklike implement features dozens of little blades that remove zest in little snowy curls. (It's also a wonderful way to grate hard cheeses, such as Parmesan and pecorino.) Just be sure not to grate any bitter white pith along with the zest.*

PASTA FROLLA

{ MAKES ONE 10-INCH PIE CRUST WITH LATTICE TOP }

This Italian short dough is a mainstay of our kitchen at Carlo's Bake Shop, where we use it in pastries such as *pasticiotti* (small custard-filled tarts) and *crostata*. To add a little more flavor, substitute ½ cup almond or pistachio flour for ½ cup all-purpose flour.

2 sticks (8 ounces) unsalted butter, softened at room temperature
1 cup granulated sugar
½ teaspoon finely grated lemon zest
½ teaspoon pure vanilla extract
½ teaspoon honey, preferably clover
1/16 teaspoon baking soda
1/16 teaspoon baking powder
¼ cup water, room temperature
2 cups all-purpose flour

1. Put the butter and sugar in the bowl of stand mixer fitted with the paddle attachment and paddle at medium speed until the butter becomes fluffy, about 3 minutes. Stop and scrape down the sides of the bowl with a rubber spatula.

2. Add the lemon zest, vanilla, honey, baking soda, and baking powder. Paddle for 1 minute, then stop and scrape.

3. Add the water and paddle at medium speed to work in the water and create a batter, about 2 minutes. Add the flour and paddle until the dough comes together, about 1 minute, taking care to not overmix.

4. Remove the dough from the bowl, form into a disc, and wrap tightly with plastic wrap. Refrigerate until well chilled, about 30 minutes.

5. Set aside one-quarter of the dough for the lattice topping. Roll out remaining dough to a 14-inch diameter and place in a 10-inch pie plate.

6. Roll out remaining dough to the same thickness and cut into six ¾-inch strips for the lattice topping.

EASTER BASKET CAKE

{ MAKES ONE 9-INCH CAKE }

This is a real showstopper that almost turns a cake into an Easter basket
with basket-weave piping on the sides, grass on top, and Easter candies, jelly beans (representing eggs),
and chocolates filling the basket on top. I've got to be honest with you, this cake isn't a walk in the park:
The basket-weave piping takes real skill and precision, so this is for more advanced cake decorators.
However, if you have some experience with a pastry bag and turntable, or are a quick study, go for it
and make this for your next Easter celebration. It's a fun, festive, unforgettable cake that might become
a tradition for your family, as it has for mine.

Two 9-inch cakes of your choosing (pages 292
    to 298)
About 3 cups white Decorator's Buttercream
    (page 302) in a pastry bag fitted with #6
    star tip
Chocolate Fudge Frosting (page 304) in a
    bag fitted with #48 interchangeable bas-
    ket weave tip
3 cups green Decorator's Buttercream (page
    302) in a piping bag fit with #233
    interchangeable grass tip
Assorted Easter candies, such as Peeps,
    Reese's peanut butter cups, and
    jelly beans, for topping the cake

a

b

d

e

1. On a turntable, prepare a double-layer cake of your choosing on a doily-lined cardboard circle, filling it with the filling of your choice and dirty icing it (a) (page 287).

2. Take the chocolate fudge bag in hand, and working from bottom to top, using the straight side of the tip (see note), pipe vertical lines around the side of the cake, ⅛-inch apart, turning the turntable after each line (b).

3. Next, starting at the bottom, and turning the turntable as you work, pipe horizontal bands over every other vertical line. Pipe another set of bands above the first set, piping them over the lines you skipped on the first level (c).

4. Continue in this fashion, piping over alternating sets of lines, until you have created a basket weave that covers the entire side of the cake (d).

5. Take the green buttercream bag in hand and squeeze-and-pull grass around the border, letting the grass come slightly over the edge. Cover the entire top of the cake with grass (e).

6. Top the cake with jelly beans, Peeps, Reese's peanut butter cups, and other candies (f).

Note: *The basket weave tip has a plain/straight side and a ruffled/serrated side.*

TEA PARTY

My daughter, Sofia, loves throwing tea parties, inviting her friends over to our home for dainty little snacks and (noncaffeinated) tea. For a guy like me, who spent my childhood doing distinctly "guy" things like playing sports in the street and local parks, it's truly enchanting to welcome a group of young girls into our home for such a refined and polite occasion. As a baker, I also love the challenge of creating a repertoire of snacks for them. This chapter includes Sofia's favorites, such as miniature cheese and cauliflower quiches, shortbread cookies that can be cut into various shapes and sizes, little scones punched up with chocolate chips, and finger sandwiches made with Nutella and bananas instead of more traditional, grown-up fillings such as goat cheese and cucumbers. And, of course, we serve a homemade berry tea and signature dessert, cookies that are decorated with fondant tea kettles. If your daughter likes hosting tea parties, these are the perfect snacks to serve; most of them can also be brought along as a contribution to a tea party at a friend's house.

CHEDDAR & CAULIFLOWER QUICHE CUTOUTS

{ SERVES 6 }

Shown here with Very Berry Tea, recipe on page 89.

I love serving little quiches to Sofia and her friends at their tea parties because there's something naturally sophisticated about this dish that seems just right for the occasion. The key for serving quiche to children is to present bite-sized pieces, punched out with little cutters in geometric shapes, or even fun, thematic shapes such as hearts or butterflies. Even children who don't normally love quiche get excited when they see them presented this way.

1 store-bought, refrigerated pie dough round (half 14.1 ounce package)

½ large head cauliflower, cut into bite-sized florets (2 heaping cups)

1 tablespoon unsalted butter

½ yellow onion, minced

6 large eggs

½ cup milk

1 cup finely shredded Cheddar cheese

1. Position a rack in the center of the oven and preheat the oven to 375°F. Unroll the pie dough out to fit into a 10-inch pie plate; prick the dough all over with a fork. Bake in the oven until light brown, about 20 minutes. Remove the plate from the oven and let cool slightly, about 10 minutes.

2. Meanwhile, pour water into a large saucepan to a depth of ½ inch, and set over medium-high heat. Add the cauliflower and cover the pan. Steam the cauliflower until tender, 10 to 12 minutes, then drain and set aside to cool slightly. Meanwhile, in a small skillet, melt the butter and heat it until foamy. Add the onion and cook, stirring often, until softened but not browned, about 4 minutes.

3. Beat the eggs in a medium bowl. Stir in the milk and cheese, season with salt and pepper, and add the slightly cooled cauliflower. Pour the mixture into the crust and bake until set, about 45 minutes. Let cool slightly, 15 to 20 minutes. Cut into shapes using biscuit cutters or deep cookie cutters, pressing firmly against the bottom of the pan if needed to push through the crust. Transfer to small plates and serve.

CHOCOLATE CHIP SCONES

{ MAKES 8 SCONES OR 24 MINIATURE SCONES }

Shown here with Simple Shortbread Cookies, recipe on page 84.

British in origin, the little quick breads called scones are a must for tea parties, although I add a touch just for kids: chocolate chips! If you'd like to make miniature scones, sized closer to some of the other items in this chapter, you can do just that.

2½ cups all-purpose flour, plus more
    for dusting
⅓ cup granulated sugar
1½ teaspoons baking powder
¼ teaspoon kosher salt
6 tablespoons cold unsalted butter,
    cut into pieces
2 large egg yolks
¾ cup half-and-half or milk, plus more for
    brushing
2 teaspoons pure vanilla extract
1⅓ cups semisweet chocolate chips
Coarse sugar, such as turbinado,
    for decorating

1. Position a rack in the center of the oven and preheat the oven to 400°F. Line a baking sheet with parchment paper.

2. In a large bowl, sift the flour, sugar, baking powder, and salt. Rub in the butter using your fingertips until it is mostly worked in and the mixture looks and feels crumbly.

3. In a separate bowl, whisk together the egg yolks, half-and-half, and vanilla extract. Add the dry ingredients to the wet, mixing just until incorporated. Stir in the chocolate chips. Gather the dough into a ball with your hands.

4. Transfer to a lightly floured surface and press into a disk about ¾-inch thick. Dip a sharp knife in flour, and use it to cut the dough into 8 equal wedges. (To make miniature scones, divide the dough into 2 discs and cut each into 8 wedges.) Transfer the wedges carefully to the prepared baking sheet, leaving about 2 inches between the scones. Brush lightly with half-and-half and dust generously with turbinado sugar. Bake until lightly browned on top and a toothpick inserted in the center comes out clean, about 20 minutes. (The scones may be kept in an airtight container at room temperature for up to 2 days.)

SIMPLE SHORTBREAD COOKIES

{ MAKES ABOUT 2 DOZEN }
Photograph on page 82.

Simple and simply elegant, shortbread cookies are a must for tea parties,
and a perfect classic counterpoint to the more complex flavors of the other options on this menu.
You can also cut these cookies into any shapes you like by using a biscuit or cookie cutter;
be careful, as the dough is delicate.

8 ounces (2 sticks) unsalted butter,
at room temperature
½ cup granulated sugar
½ teaspoon pure vanilla extract
⅛ teaspoon fine salt
2 cups all-purpose flour, plus more for
sprinkling dough

1. Put the butter, sugar, vanilla, and salt in a bowl and beat until the mixture is light and fluffy. Stir in the flour until just incorporated.

2. Turn the dough out onto a large piece of plastic wrap; use the plastic wrap to help form the dough into a rectangle, about ¾-inch thick. Wrap tightly in the plastic wrap and refrigerate for at least 2 hours. (The dough may be refrigerated for up to 2 days.)

3. Line a baking sheet with parchment paper, position a rack in the center of the oven, and preheat the oven to 325°F. Unwrap the dough and transfer to a lightly floured work surface; sprinkle the top of the dough lightly with flour. Gently roll the dough using a rolling pin to about ½-inch thick. Slice into 2 inch x 2-inch squares. Prick the centers with a fork.

4. Bake until just beginning to brown on the edges, about 15 minutes. Let cool on the baking sheet about 10 minutes, then transfer to wire racks to cool completely. (The cookies may be kept in an airtight container at room temperature for up to 2 days.)

STRAWBERRY TOASTER PASTRY

{ MAKES 12 SMALL PASTRIES }

Because I come from a family of professional bakers, I never understood why all my friends loved Pop-Tarts. I don't have anything against them, but they don't compare to something freshly baked and frosted. The thing that really skeeved me was how many kids I knew who didn't even heat them, but instead ate them cold and hard, right from the package. When my own children started asking me about Pop-Tarts, because all their friends love them, too (cycle of life, I guess), I decided to whip up a homemade version to show them how I'd go about making this treat. Now, when my kids' friends are over, and they ask for Pop-Tarts for breakfast, this is what we make for them.

All-purpose flour, for dusting
2 rounds refrigerated pie crust dough
    (one 14.1ounce package) or see recipe for
    Piecrust dough (page 223) and double it
Strawberry jam
1 large egg
1 cup confectioners' sugar
½ teaspoon pure vanilla extract
Kosher salt
Sprinkles, optional

1. Position a rack in the center of the oven and preheat the oven to 375°F. Line a baking sheet with aluminum foil or parchment paper.

2. Lightly flour a work surface and unroll the pie crusts. Lightly flour a rolling pin and roll over the crusts with the rolling pin a few times to smooth and stretch the dough. Cut each round of pie dough into twelve 2-inch by 3-inch rectangles, discarding the rounded pieces of dough remaining on the edges.

3. Transfer 6 of the rectangles to a baking sheet and fill with 1½ teaspoons of the strawberry jam. Lightly spread the jam with the back of a teaspoon or a rubber spatula, leaving a slim border around the edges of the dough. Beat the egg in a small bowl and add about 1 tablespoon water. Brush the edges of the dough with the beaten egg, and top with another sheet of dough. Press down with the tines of a fork to seal.

4. Bake until lightly golden brown and flaky, 12 to 14 minutes. Remove the sheet from the oven and let pastry cool slightly.

5. Meanwhile, put the confectioners' sugar, 3 teaspoons of water, the vanilla extract, and a small pinch salt in a small bowl and stir together. Drizzle the glaze onto the tarts, and top with a scattering of sprinkles, if desired.

NUTELLA & BANANA FINGER SANDWICHES

{ MAKES 8 }

My daughter, Sofia, *loves* the chocolate-hazelnut spread Nutella, and especially loves it with bananas, so I'm always looking for ways to combine the two. When she hosted one of her tea parties, I decided to use Nutella in a decadent play on tea sandwiches. Usually tea sandwiches would have something savory, such as cucumbers, inside. These have Nutella and bananas and—on top of that—are griddled to fuse the flavors.

These are messy to make and messier to eat, but that's one of the reasons kids love them!

4 slices Italian or other rustic white
    sandwich bread
¼ cup chocolate-hazelnut spread,
    such as Nutella
1 large or 2 small firm-ripe bananas
2 tablespoons unsalted butter
Confectioners' sugar, for dusting

1. Using a sharp knife, evenly slice the crusts off the bread to form a square or rectangle. Working with two at a time on your cutting board, cut the bread slices into four triangles by cutting an "x" through them. Repeat with the remaining slices.

2. Using an offset spatula or small rubber spatula, gently spread the insides of the triangles (tops and bottoms) with a thin layer of the Nutella, keeping the edges of the bread clean. Cut the banana on a bias to form long slices; lay one long slice in each sandwich.

3. Melt the butter on a griddle or in a large nonstick skillet over medium-low heat. When foaming, add the sandwiches to the pan (do not crowd the pan; work in batches if necessary). Cook, pressing down with your spatula or fingers only once, at the beginning, until the bread is lightly toasted, 2 to 3 minutes. Carefully flip the sandwiches, and cook until lightly toasted on the other side, 2 to 3 minutes more.

4. Transfer to plates and dust the sandwiches with confectioners' sugar to serve.

VERY BERRY TEA

{ SERVES 4 TO 6 }
Photograph on page 80.

You can't have a tea party without tea! There's just one thing: A lot of parents don't like serving their children caffeinated drinks, and a lot of kids don't like the taste of traditional tea.

The solution? A berry-flavored herbal tea that's sweetened with homemade simple syrup and chilled. Regardless of the nature of this kid-friendly tea, be sure to serve it in adult tea cups or it won't be a real tea party.

¼ cup granulated sugar
3 bags herbal mixed berry tea (decaffeinated)
½ cup cranberry-raspberry juice
¼ cup fresh blueberries

1. Put the sugar and ¼ cup water in a small, heavy saucepan. Bring to a boil, stirring with a wooden spoon, until the sugar dissolves. Transfer the simple syrup to a heatproof glass or small bowl and refrigerate until cool.

2. Meanwhile, brew the tea: Add the tea bags to 4 cups boiling water and let stand about 3 minutes. Discard the bags; let cool slightly, then refrigerate until chilled.

3. When ready to serve, combine the cranberry-raspberry juice, the chilled tea, and the cooled sugar mixture to taste in a glass teapot or small pitcher. Serve the tea chilled, in teacups, garnished with the fresh blueberries.

TEA KETTLE COOKIES

{ MAKES 10 TO 12 COOKIES }

My daughter, Sofia, loves making these cookies with me whenever she hosts a tea party. They echo the theme of the festivities with a simple fondant tea kettle applied to a rectangular cookie. You don't have to use the same colors that I do here, or pipe the tea kettle accents exactly the way I do; feel free to express yourself by drawing those bits in your own style, or letting your kids go to town.

Sugar Cookies (page 189), cut into 10 to
    12 cookies, 3-inches by 4-inches each
2 cups white Decorator's Buttercream
    (page 302)
12 ounces yellow fondant (1 ounce
    per cookie)
1½ pounds purple fondant (2 ounces
    per cookie)
12 ounces pink fondant
2 cups pink Decorator's Buttercream in a
    pastry bag fitted with #3 plain tip or in a
    parchment pencil (page 39)

TOOLS & EQUIPMENT
X-ACTO knife, or sharp-thin bladed knife,
    such as a paring knife
Ruler
Tea kettle cookie cutter
Water pen
Extra-small daisy plunger cutter
    (flower-shaped cutter)

a

b

c

d

1. Use an icing spatula to spread a thin layer of buttercream onto the top of each cookie. (Lay the cookies on your work surface to do this; if you hold them in your hand as you ice them, they may break **(a)**.

2. Roll the yellow fondant out to ⅛-inch thick and cut twelve 3-inch by 4-inch rectangles out of it using a ruler to guide you. Set 1 rectangle atop the frosting on each cookie and press down gently but firmly to make sure it adheres **(b)**. Roll the purple fondant out to ⅛-inch thick. Punch out 12 tea kettles with the cookie cutter **(c)**.

3. Roll the pink fondant out ⅛-inch thick and punch out 12 flowers with the daisy cutter.

4. Use the water pen to apply water to one side of each tea kettle and set it on the yellow fondant on each cookie, pressing down gently. Dab water onto one side of each flower and place 1 at the top of each tea kettle **(d)**.

5. Pipe pink frosting in a wavy line at the top of each tea kettle, 7 small dots above it, and 1 dot in the center of the flower **(e)**. Pipe a wavy line to accentuate the spout and another one to accentuate the bottom of the kettle, then the handle. Pipe 4 small dots below the line at the base of the kettle.

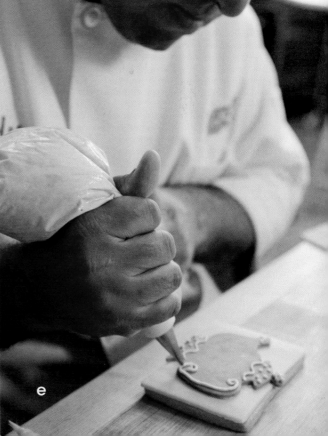

e

KID'S BIRTHDAY PARTY

There are few things I look forward to more than my kids' birthday parties, or any kids' birthday parties for that matter. When a child knows that a day is "his" or "hers," it's great fun to watch them soak up the attention and enjoy the company of their best friends. My philosophy when it comes to the menu is to spoil them rotten with all the things that kids love: popcorn coated with white chocolate and sprinkles, miniature pizza puffs stuffed with cheese and pepperoni, sesame chicken fingers, and brownie sundaes. (For a nod to healthfulness, I also sneak in crunchy broccoli with Parmesan and breadcrumbs.) Of course, the cake is the focal point of any birthday party, and the one presented here features a jersey on top—it can be adapted to reflect the birthday boy or girl's favorite sports team, rock band, organization, or club, making the guest of honor feel like the center of attention on his or her special day.

WHITE CHOCOLATE BIRTHDAY POPCORN

{ SERVES 6 TO 8 }

One of my favorite things about going to the movies is the snacks—popcorn, candy, chocolate … I love it all, and sometimes I can't make up my mind. As a kid, I used to buy all three, put the chocolate and candy in the popcorn box, and mix them together, letting the chocolate melt over the popcorn. That memory inspired this chocolate and rainbow-sprinkles–coated popcorn.

Be sure to use a high-quality chocolate or it won't melt properly.

One 4-ounce bar good-quality white
    chocolate, coarsely chopped
6 cups popped, lightly salted popcorn
    (no butter)
¼ cup rainbow sprinkles
Kosher salt

1. Put the chocolate in a heatproof bowl and set it over a pot of simmering water (do not let the bowl touch the water); cook, stirring frequently, until melted.

2. Add the popcorn to an extra-large bowl (or divide between 2 large bowls), and spoon the melted white chocolate over it in batches, tossing to coat after each addition. Sprinkle with 2 tablespoons of the sprinkles and a pinch of salt, tossing to incorporate.

3. Line 2 baking sheets with aluminum foil and spread the popcorn out over them in a single layer. Sprinkle with the remaining 2 tablespoons sprinkles. Let stand until cooled and set, about 2 hours. The popcorn is best served right away, but can be stored in a cold place or refrigerated (to keep the chocolate from melting) in an airtight container for 24 hours.

PEPPERONI PIZZA PUFFS

{ MAKES 8 }

Shown here with Baked Broccoli Bites and Sesame Chicken Fingers, recipes on pages 100 and 101.

Pizza seems like a great party food, but it can be a little messy and also gets cold fast. One year, for a birthday party for one of the cousins, my brother-in-law Joey, who's always been a creative problem solver, had the idea to make pizza puffs, putting the filling inside the dough, in a sort of mini-calzone. As with pizza, you can change the filling, replacing the pepperoni with sausage or vegetables, such as sautéed mushrooms.

One 16 ounce ball frozen pizza dough
(see note), thawed in the refrigerator for
6 hours, then left out to rise in oiled bowl,
covered with plastic wrap, at room temperature for 2 hours
All-purpose flour, for dusting
½ cup shredded or fresh sliced mozzarella
24 thin slices pepperoni
1 jarred red pepper, drained and cut into
1½-inch strips
About 2 tablespoons olive oil

1. Position a rack in the center of the oven and preheat the oven to 425°F. Line a baking sheet with aluminum foil.

2. Cut the dough into 8 equal pieces. Using floured hands if needed, carefully stretch each piece into a thin disk (the shape doesn't have to be perfect) about 5 inches in diameter.

3. Transfer the dough balls to the prepared baking sheet and fill each with ½ tablespoon mozzarella on one half, leaving a 1-inch border around the edge. Line the cheese with 3 slices pepperoni, and a strip of red pepper. Starting from the smaller border, stretch the dough over the filling, then continue rolling the dough (like you would roll a carpet) to wrap the filling twice. Place on a foil-lined baking sheet, seam-side down. Pinch any holes with your fingers to patch.

4. Brush the dough with a very light coating of olive oil. Bake until golden-brown, 15 to 17 minutes, then remove from the oven and let rest for 5 minutes before serving.

Dough the Right Thing: *Many supermarkets sell pizza dough these days, but there's nothing like the real thing, freshly made by a pizzaiola (pizza maker). Most pizza shops will be happy to sell you some of their dough and I suggest that you get it from them when you want to make a pizza.*

BAKED BROCCOLI BITES

{ SERVES 4 TO 6 }
Photograph on page 98.

We all want to let our kids do whatever they want at their birthday parties, and usually that means nothing but junk food. But, even on an anything-goes occasion, there's still room for a little moderation. These broccoli bites are easy to make and packed with flavor and texture from the breadcrumbs and Parmesan, and are baked rather than fried.

2 large eggs
½ teaspoon kosher salt
1 cup plain dry breadcrumbs
Freshly ground black pepper
1 tablespoon finely grated Parmesan
12 ounces broccoli florets, cut into bite-size
    pieces, long stems trimmed
1 tablespoon olive oil
Ranch dressing, for serving

1. Position a rack in the center of the oven and preheat the oven to 375°F. Line a baking sheet with aluminum foil.

2. Make an egg wash by beating the eggs with 2 teaspoons water; season with ¼ teaspoon salt. Fill large resealable plastic bag or bowl with the breadcrumbs. Season the crumbs with the remaining ¼ teaspoon salt and a few grinds of black pepper, then stir in the Parmesan.

3. Toss the broccoli into the egg mixture to coat the florets. Using a fork, transfer to the breadcrumbs, first letting any excess egg drip off. Toss to coat well in the breadcrumbs. Transfer the broccoli to the prepared baking sheet. Drizzle with the olive oil, tossing gently to coat, then spread the broccoli out in an even layer. Bake until the breadcrumbs are golden brown and crispy and the broccoli has softened slightly, about 15 minutes, gently shaking the pan occasionally to prevent scorching, and cook evenly. Let cool slightly. Transfer to a bowl or platter, and serve with ranch dressing for dipping.

SESAME CHICKEN FINGERS

{ SERVES 6 }

Photograph on page 98.

On some weeknights, my family gets together spontaneously for dinner at one of our homes: Sometimes Lisa and I host; sometimes it's Mauro and Madeline, or Joey and Grace. Because we're all so busy, we often order in, usually from one of the Italian-American restaurants in the area. Once in a while, however, we change it up and order Chinese food. All the kids love sesame chicken, so when one of the cousins has a birthday, this adaptation is always on the menu.

Nonstick cooking spray or canola oil
1¼ pounds chicken breast, cut into
    2-inch strips (about 12 strips)
Kosher salt
1¼ cups panko breadcrumbs
1 tablespoon sesame oil
1 cup teriyaki sauce
2 tablespoons rice vinegar
⅔ cup honey
1 teaspoon cornstarch
1 tablespoon sesame seeds
2 tablespoons chopped scallion greens

1. Preheat the oven to 425°F. Line a baking sheet with aluminum foil, then lightly coat with cooking spray or brush with canola oil.

2. Season the chicken with salt, then roll in the panko crumbs, pressing to adhere. Place on the prepared baking sheet without crowding, and bake until the chicken is cooked through, about 20 minutes (the breadcrumbs will not be browned deeply).

3. Meanwhile, put the sesame oil, teriyaki, vinegar, and honey in a small, heavy saucepan, and bring to a boil over high heat. Cook, stirring occasionally, until reduced by half, about 10 minutes. Stir in the cornstarch and boil 1 minute more until the sauce is thick enough to coat the back of a spoon. Remove the pan from the heat and let cool slightly.

4. Pour half the sauce into a large bowl, then add half the chicken strips, and toss the chicken in the sauce to coat. Sprinkle with half the sesame seeds. Transfer those strips to a serving platter, and repeat with the remaining sauce and chicken. Scatter the scallions over the chicken and serve.

CANDY BAR BROWNIE SUNDAES

{ SERVES 8 }

These sundaes are pure decadence, with homemade brownies, chopped-up candy bars, and ice cream in the same bowl. I got the idea for them when watching my kids at a frozen yogurt chain—they love walking down the line with their cup of yogurt and piling on as many different toppings as possible. If you like, put all the ingredients for these sundaes out in bowls, and let each child make his or her own sundae.

6 ounces semisweet chocolate, coarsely chopped

6 ounces (1½ sticks) cup unsalted butter, plus more for greasing the pan

3 large eggs

1 cup granulated sugar

1 teaspoon pure vanilla extract

½ cup plus 2 tablespoons all-purpose flour

¾ teaspoon baking powder

⅛ teaspoon kosher salt

2 pints vanilla ice cream

4 candy bars, of different kinds, cut with a sharp, heavy knife into bite-sized pieces

Whipped cream, for serving

Maraschino cherries, drained, for serving

1. Make the brownies: Put the chocolate and butter in a heatproof bowl and set it over a pot of simmering water (do not let the bowl touch the water); cook, stirring frequently, until the chocolate and butter are melted and smooth. Set aside to cool slightly.

2. Meanwhile, position a rack in the center of the oven and preheat the oven to 350°F. Butter a 9-inch square glass or metal baking pan and line it with parchment paper.

3. In a separate bowl, stir together the eggs, sugar, and vanilla. Stir in the slightly cooled chocolate mixture. Set the bowl aside and let the mixture cool almost completely.

4. In a small bowl, stir together the flour, baking powder, and salt. Stir the dry ingredients into the wet, mixing just to incorporate between additions.

5. Pour the mixture into the prepared pan and bake until the top is dry and a toothpick inserted in the center comes out clean, about 40 minutes. Remove and let cool until firm and cool enough to work with by hand, about 20 minutes. Remove from the pan using the parchment sheet to help you; discard the parchment and transfer to a rack to finish cooling (or serve warm if desired). Cut into 8 large brownies. (The brownies are best right away, but may be stored in an airtight container for up to 2 days.)

6. When ready to serve, place 1 brownie in the bottom of each of 8 serving bowls. Top with 1 large or two small scoops ice cream. Sprinkle with the candy pieces, top with a little whipped cream and a maraschino cherry.

BIRTHDAY PARTY JERSEY CAKE

{ MAKES ONE 9-INCH CAKE }

Cakes don't need to be over the top to make a child happy. For a birthday cake, the main thing is to prepare something that makes the center of attention feel special. I can't tell you how many kids I've seen light up when we present them with a cake that has a jersey with the colors of their favorite pro sports team, or their school team, and the number of their favorite player, or their own number, on it. For kids who aren't sports fans, you can use this same design to celebrate an organization or club, school colors, or even a rock band.

Two 9-inch cakes of your choosing (pages 292 to 298), filled with your choice of filling (pages 302 to 311)

4 cups white Decorator's Buttercream (page 302) in a pastry bag fitted with #6 star tip

30 ounces white fondant

6 ounces red fondant

6 ounces blue fondant

About 1 cup red Decorator's Buttercream in a pastry bag fitted with #6 plain tip

TOOLS & EQUIPMENT

Rolling pin

Poker

Letter impression set

Large and medium star cutters

Fondant ribbon cutter

Steamer (see Tip, page 107)

X-ACTO knife or sharp, thin-bladed knife such as a paring knife

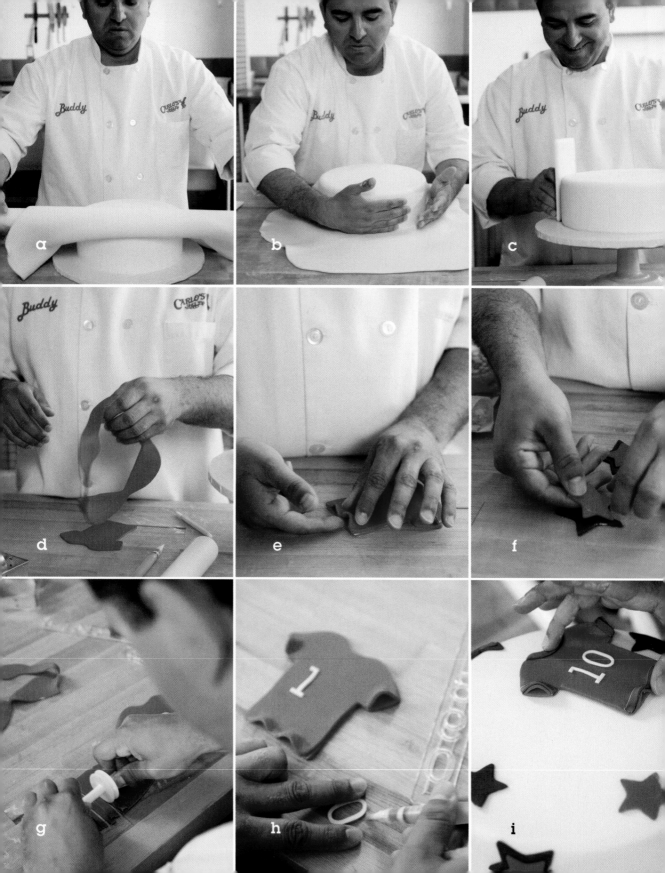

a

b

c

d

e

f

g

h

i

1. On a turntable, prepare a double-layer cake on a doiley-lined cardboard circle, filling it with the filling of your choice and dirty icing it without the tip (page 287). (Note: After dirty-icing it, keep white buttercream in the bag for affixing design elements to the cake and creating the shell border.)

    Drape the cake with white fondant (a, b), smooth it in place with the smoother (c), and trim it (page 289). Do not return the fondant to the tub; you will need it for the jersey numbers.

2. Roll the red fondant out to ⅛-inch thickness. Cut a jersey using a pizza wheel or X-ACTO knife, or make a cardboard template and use it as a guide (d). Cut another jersey of the same shape and size. Use a water pen to glue the two jerseys together, crimping the top layer at the sleeves and bottom to create a three-dimensional effect (e).

3. Punch out 3 large stars and 6 medium stars from the remaining red fondant using the star cutters. Roll out the blue fondant to ⅛ inch thick and punch out 3 large stars and 6 medium stars. Use a water pen to affix 3 medium red stars to 3 large blue stars and 3 medium blue stars to 3 large red stars (f).

4. Cut strips of blue fondant ¼-inch wide with a strip cutter (g) to make trim for the neck, shoulder, and bottom of the jersey (size will vary based on your jersey size). Trim the strips to size with an X-ACTO knife, and affix to the jersey with the water pen.

5. Punch out the numbers and use a water pen to affix them to the jersey (h).

6. Steam the cake with the steamer.

7. Apply the jersey to the top of the cake (if you want to write a birthday message, position the jersey to one side). Then add the stars to the top and sides of the cake (i).

8. Steam the cake again, paying particular attention to the jersey and stars, to make the elements look clean and shiny.

9. Using the red buttercream, rotate the turntable and pipe a small shell border around the bottom of the cake (j).

Tip: *If you do not have a steamer, you can apply all design elements with a water pen, although the steamer will make the cake and those elements look dramatically sharper and shinier.*

MOTHER'S DAY BREAKFAST IN BED

I've been blessed to have two incredible mothers in my life: My own mother, who I've lived with through great times and bad my entire life, and who did a fabulous job raising me and my four sisters, and of course my wife, Lisa, who's an amazing mother to our four beautiful children. I'm in awe of Lisa every day and try to show my appreciation in little ways whenever I can. But on Mother's Day, I go all out, involving the kids in the preparation of a special breakfast that we deliver to Lisa in bed. (Later in the day, my mother comes to the house and we visit with her.) The dishes here hit all the buttons: an egg dish made with basil and fontina cheese, blueberry lemon pancakes, and bacon baked with maple syrup. There are two choices for desserts, a berry tartlet and a Mother's Day Volcano Mousse Cake—both sized as individual treats that can fit on a breakfast tray, although—like everything in this chapter—these dishes can also be served at the table for a family extravaganza.

BASIL EGG STRATA

{ SERVES 4 TO 6 }

Lisa loves egg dishes, so there's always an egg dish on the menu on Mother's Day. This strata is one of her favorites—a meal on its own in some respects, with bread, cheese, and vegetables all baked together. I especially love the inclusion of basil, which makes us all think of summer, which is just around the corner on Mother's Day.

This strata is a perfect Mother's Day main course and also terrific for entertaining, because the casserole can be prepared the day before you plan to bake and serve it.

1 tablespoon butter, plus more for
   greasing the pan
1 small yellow onion, chopped (about 1 cup)
¼ teaspoon kosher salt
Freshly ground black pepper
8 large eggs
⅓ cup milk
4 cups bread cubes (about 1 inch) cut from
   a hearty loaf, such as a baguette
1½ cups (about 4 ounces) shredded
   fontina cheese
¾ cup fresh basil, chopped

1. In a saucepan over medium-high heat, heat 1 tablespoon butter until foamy, then add the onion and season with ⅛ teaspoon of salt and a few grinds of pepper. Cook, stirring often, until the onion is softened, 4 to 5 minutes.

2. Transfer the onion to a heatproof mixing bowl. Whisk in the eggs, milk, remaining ⅛ teaspoon of salt, and pepper.

3. Grease a 9-inch square glass baking dish with butter. Add half of the bread cubes in a layer on the bottom of the dish. Top evenly with half the fontina, then half the basil. Pour on half the egg mixture. Repeat the layering once, starting with the remaining bread cubes. Then toss all gently in the pan to help thoroughly coat the ingredients with the egg. Cover with plastic wrap and refrigerate at least 1½ hours, or overnight, to help the bread absorb the egg mixture. Let stand at room temperature 30 minutes before baking.

4. Position a rack in the center of the oven and preheat the oven to 325°F. Bake until the top of the strata is lightly browned and the middle no longer looks runny when pierced with a knife, about 45 minutes. Serve warm, cut into squares.

BLUEBERRY-LEMON PANCAKES

{ SERVES 4 }

Shown here with Maple-Glazed Bacon and Chai Tea Lattes, recipes on pages 114 and 115.

If you've never made pancakes from scratch, do yourself a favor and try this recipe. You may never use a ready-made mix again. Coming from a family of bakers, we never used a mix—we don't use a mix for *anything*—but the thing about pancakes is that they don't require any finesse – you just mix the ingredients and make them the same way you've made them all your life.

These pancakes with blueberries and lemon are Lisa's favorite. You can leave out either or both, or leave out the lemon and replace the blueberries with chocolate chips.

1 cup plus 2 tablespoons all-purpose or
   white whole-wheat flour
½ teaspoon baking powder
½ teaspoon baking soda
1 teaspoon granulated sugar
Kosher salt
1 cup buttermilk
1 large egg
1 tablespoon plus 2 teaspoons vegetable oil
1 teaspoon pure vanilla extract
1 cup fresh blueberries
¼ teaspoon finely grated lemon zest
1½ tablespoons unsalted butter
Pure maple syrup, for serving

1. Put the flour, baking powder, baking soda, sugar, and a pinch of salt in a large bowl and stir them together.

2. In a separate bowl, whisk together the buttermilk, egg, vegetable oil, and vanilla. Working in two or three batches, whisk the dry ingredients into the wet until the mixture looks smooth. Stir in the blueberries and lemon zest.

3. Preheat a large nonstick pan or griddle over medium-high heat. Add about ½ tablespoon butter and heat until foamy. Slowly ladle in ¼ cup scoops of the batter, leaving about 1 inch between pancakes. Cook until pancakes are lightly golden brown on the bottom and bubbling on the top, two to three minutes. Flip and cook until lightly browned on the other side, 1 to 2 minutes.

4. Transfer to plates and repeat with the remaining batter, using more butter as needed to coat the pan. Top pancakes with maple syrup.

MAPLE-GLAZED BACON

{ SERVES 4 }

Photograph on page 113.

Bacon is a perfect ingredient: It makes the ultimate side dish on its own, and adds great, smoky flavor to anything you cook it with. But you can make bacon even better by slowly cooking it with maple syrup and black pepper, adding even more flavor. In addition to serving this for breakfast, it's a wonderful side dish with barbecued meats.

8 slices smoked bacon
About ¼ cup pure maple syrup
Freshly ground black pepper

1. Position a rack in the center of the oven and preheat the oven to 350°F. Set a large cooling rack over a rimmed baking sheet, or line a rimmed baking sheet with two layers of parchment paper.

2. Using a pastry brush or your fingers, coat the bacon slices on both sides with some of the maple syrup. Sprinkle generously with freshly ground black pepper. Lay the slices side by side on the baking rack or baking sheet (they can be close together, but should not be touching). Bake until deep brown and crispy, 10 to 12 minutes. Dab with a paper towel to remove some of the grease if desired. Serve hot.

The Ultimate: *To really put this over the top, use the best bacon possible (like the artisanal version made by Nueske's) and grade B maple syrup.*

CHAI TEA LATTES

{ SERVES 4 }

Photograph on page 113.

I'm a straight coffee and espresso drinker, and so is my wife, Lisa.
However, my sister Grace has jumped on the bandwagon of every trendy coffee drink that comes along.
Most recently, she's fallen in love with chai lattes, made with an aromatic blend of spices and tea. (I have
to say, when I finally got around to tasting one, I thought it was delicious—a baker's brew if ever there
were such a thing.) Here's a simple recipe for making chai latte at home.

2 tablespoons loose black tea
    (or 4 black teabags)
2 cloves
2 whole cardamom pods
1 cinnamon stick
1 teaspoon ground ginger
¼ teaspoon pure vanilla extract
1¼ cups milk
1 tablespoon granulated sugar

1. Bring 3 cups of water to a boil in a small
   saucepan. Pour the water into a teapot,
   large bowl, or quart-sized jar, then stir in the
   black tea, cloves, cardamom, cinnamon, and
   ginger. Let steep, stirring occasionally, 3 to 5
   minutes.

2. Meanwhile, put the vanila, milk, and sugar in
   the same saucepan and cook over medium
   heat until hot, whisking occasionally to help
   the sugar incorporate.

3. Strain the tea mixture into four mugs; then
   divide the sweetened milk among the mugs.
   Serve hot.

SUGAR-DUSTED BLACKBERRY TARTLETS

{ SERVES 4 }

Once in a while, when Lisa and I were dating, I'd surprise her by making her something that wasn't part of our repertoire at Carlo's Bake Shop. One of the treats she loved most was a little tartlet topped with blackberries and powdered sugar. It's more French than Italian or American in style and, because of that, it's naturally romantic. To this day, I make these for her once in a while, and always serve one to her on Mother's Day.

6 tablespoons unsalted butter, softened
¼ cup granulated sugar
1 large egg
½ teaspoon almond extract
1 cup all-purpose flour
2 tablespoons oats
Scant pinch kosher salt
1 cup heavy cream
1 pint fresh blackberries
Confectioners' sugar, for dusting

1. Position a rack in the center of the oven and preheat to 375°F.

2. In the bowl of a stand mixer, beat the butter and granulated sugar together on medium-high speed, about 1 minute. Add the egg and the almond extract and beat to incorporate. Add the flour, oats, and salt and mix on low speed until the wet and dry ingredients are just combined. Gather the dough into a ball using your fingers, then remove and cut the dough into 4 equal pieces.

3. Place 1 piece of dough in the center of a 3 by 5-inch mini-tart pan with a removable bottom. Press with your fingers to distribute it evenly across the bottom and sides of the pan in a thin (¼-inch-thick) layer. (Be careful not to overhandle or the dough will become sticky and thin.) Trim any excess dough that hangs over the sides of the pan and discard. Repeat with three more tart pans and the remaining three dough pieces, transferring the finished tart shells to the refrigerator while you work on the others.

4. Transfer the tart pans to a baking sheet and prick all over with a fork. Bake 10 minutes, checking to see if the dough has puffed up in the pan (if it has, press it down gently against the bottom of the pan with a fork). Bake again until golden brown, 12 to 15 minutes. Let cool completely.

5. Meanwhile, whip the cream using an electric mixer until stiff peaks form. Fill each tart shell with whipped cream; do not overfill, as you'll be topping with the berries. Top each with 6 to 8 blackberries. Dust the finished tart with confectioners' sugar and serve immediately.

MOTHER'S DAY VOLCANO MOUSSE CAKE

{ MAKES 12 CAKES }

Like the Spiky Layer Cake on page 55, these insanely moist, potently chocolate desserts can be successfully made with kids helping out, and don't require a lot of finesse. They are also single serve, and scaled to fit perfectly on a breakfast-in-bed tray, leaving plenty of extras for the rest of the family, or for visitors. (You can also take them along to another home, or to a grand-mother's house.)

12 chocolate muffins (Chocolate Cake batter baked in a muffin tin with ½ cup, 2-inch-deep wells)

7 cups (double the recipe) My Dad's Chocolate Mousse (page 308)

8 cups (quadruple the recipe) Chocolate Ganache (page 309)

12 large strawberries, cut in half lengthwise

About 6 ounces store-bought chocolate shavings

TOOLS & EQUIPMENT
Pastry bag fitted with #6 star tip

1. Use a small, sharp knife, such as a paring knife, to carve a small, inverted-cone-shaped hole, about 1-inch deep, out of the top of each muffin (a). (Discard or snack on the cut-out cake.) Use a cake spatula to fill the hole in each muffin with chocolate mousse, spreading it level with the top of the muffin (b). Arrange the muffins on a parchment-lined baking tray, and freeze them for at least 2 hours or up to 24 hours. Put the remaining chocolate mousse in a pastry bag fitted with #6 star tip and refrigerate until ready to finish and serve the volcanoes.

2. Have 12 small dessert plates at the ready: Melt the chocolate ganache and pour it into a heatproof bowl. When the ganache has cooled just enough to be safe to touch, dip 1 volcano into the ganache at a time, turning it to coat it (c). (As you can see in these pictures, I use my hands (d), but suggest you use slotted spoons or wooden spoons for safety.) Transfer the volcano to the center of a plate, mousse side down. For a more formal effect, set each volcano on a small round board.

3. Working with 1 volcano at a time, pipe a swirl of chocolate mousse on top. Rotating the plate on your work surface like a turntable, pipe small swirls around the base of the volcano (e). Top each volcano with the halves of 1 strawberry (f), and stick chocolate shavings in the mousse around the base.

MEMORIAL DAY GRILLING CLASSICS

Summer may not officially begin until the solstice on June 21 but, for my money, the season kicks off at the end of May with Memorial Day. That's when we uncover the pool, turn up the tunes, and get our friends and family together for a big party. Of course, from a food standpoint, one of the highlights of summer is grilling, so for our Memorial Day celebration, everything gets cooked outside over an open flame: seafood, chicken, even the fruits for dessert. Watching your food get cooked outside, and the anticipation for the moment when the grill master says, "Come and get it!" are two of my favorite summer moments, and the char flavor that a grill imparts on the food is something you just can't get by cooking indoors. This chapter features a bunch of my favorite grilled dishes, as well as a cake shaped like a grill that is the perfect way to end any summer party, from the first one on Memorial Day to the last one at summer's end in early September.

BARBECUED CHICKEN WINGS WITH HOMEMADE SAUCE

{ SERVES 8 }

Shown here with Prosciutto-Wrapped Asparagus, recipe on page 126.

If you are lucky enough to live in, or have traveled to, a hub of great barbecue, it can change your view of this food forever. For me, the standard by which all barbecue is measured is Oklahoma Joe's, a restaurant inside a gas station in Kansas City, where they serve barbecue with such a perfect balance of smoke and spice that I can still taste it today. Memories of that 'cue inspired these wings and their homemade sauce, a million times better than anything you can buy in a bottle or jar.

1 cup ketchup
¼ cup cider vinegar
⅓ cup brown sugar
¾ teaspoon Worcestershire
1 tablespoon molasses
½ teaspoon kosher salt, plus more for
    seasoning the chicken
½ teaspoon onion powder
½ teaspoon freshly ground black pepper
½ teaspoon ground mustard
⅛ teaspoon cayenne pepper
3½ to 4 pounds chicken wingettes
    and drumettes (about 24 pieces)

1. Put the ketchup, cider vinegar, brown sugar, Worcestershire, molasses, salt, onion powder, black pepper, mustard, cayenne pepper, and 2 tablespoons water in a medium, heavy saucepan and set over low heat. Cook, stirring frequently with a wooden spoon until the sugar melts and the flavors meld, about 5 minutes. Pour the sauce into a bowl, and chill until ready to use.

2. When ready to cook and serve the chicken, preheat grill to medium-low heat.

3. Season the chicken lightly with salt and place on the grates. Cook, turning as needed, until the outsides are lightly charred and crispy and the insides are cooked through, about 20 minutes for wingettes and 24 minutes for drumettes. Baste the wings with the sauce on the grill and cook 1 minute more, or transfer them to a bowl, add the sauce, and toss.

4. Transfer the wings to a serving platter or individual plates and serve.

PROSCIUTTO-WRAPPED ASPARAGUS

{ SERVES 4 }
Photograph on page 124.

Wrapping asparagus in prosciutto and grilling it fuses the two together. The most popular prosciutto-wrapped foods are probably shrimp and scallops, but I especially love prosciutto-wrapped asparagus for the contrast between the salty meat and the clean, crisp vegetable. This is another one of those recipes that Lisa turns to in order to get the kids to eat their vegetables.

12 asparagus spears, trimmed
1 tablespoon olive oil or canola oil
Kosher salt
Freshly ground pepper
12 thin slices prosciutto

1. Preheat a grill to medium heat.

2. Meanwhile, on a large platter or small baking sheet, toss the asparagus with the oil; season lightly with salt and pepper.

3. Working with one spear at a time, wrap a piece of prosciutto around the center of each asparagus, leaving the tips and ends exposed. Grill, turning carefully but frequently, until the asparagus is crisp-tender and the meat is lightly browned in places, 8 to 10 minutes.

4. Artfully arrange the prosciutto-wrapped spears on a platter and serve.

GRILLED FRUIT SKEWERS

{ MAKES 8 SKEWERS }
Photograph on page 128.

Grilling fruit isn't a natural thing to do. Fresh, juicy fruit doesn't seem to belong on the same equipment we use to char meats and do our barbecuing. But on an island vacation, we fell in love with grilled fruit, which were served on little skewers poolside at our hotel. Dressing them with butter and grilling them over high heat really brings out the maximum natural sweetness, caramelizing them. And serving them on skewers makes them the ultimate entertaining treat.

2 tablespoons unsalted butter, melted

2 tablespoons orange juice, preferably freshly squeezed or *not* from concentrate

1 tablespoon maple syrup

Kosher salt

Freshly ground pepper

⅛ teaspoon dried thyme

1½ quarts strawberries, hulled

6 firm-ripe kiwis, peeled and sliced ½-inch thick (about 4 slices per kiwi)

3 firm-ripe nectarines, cut into thick wedges

⅔ of a cored pineapple, coarsely diced

1. In a medium bowl, whisk together the melted butter, orange juice, maple syrup, a pinch of salt, a pinch of pepper, and the dried thyme.

2. Preheat a grill to medium-low. Skewer the fruit onto metal or presoaked bamboo skewers, alternating the order of the pieces. Brush with the butter mixture.

3. Grill the fruit skewers over direct heat, turning once or twice, until charred in spots and lightly caramelized, about 2 minutes per side. Serve warm.

Grate Expectations: *It's always important to scrape your grill clean before and after cooking anything on it, but especially important before grilling these skewers. You don't want the flavor of various meats to interfere with that of the fruit.*

SCALLOP & BELL PEPPER KEBABS

{ SERVES 4 }

Shown here with Grilled Fruit Skewers, recipe on page 127.

This recipe is based on one that Lisa and I make on the grill when we entertain in the summer. I love the way the sweet, crunchy pepper offers a contrast to the rich, meaty scallops. Scallops can be tricky to turn because they are so delicate; you might want to use a large spatula or tongs to help you turn them on the grill.

¼ cup freshly squeezed lemon juice
(from about 2 large lemons)
¼ cup plus 2 tablespoons olive oil
1 large clove garlic, thinly sliced
1 sprig fresh or 1 teaspoon dried rosemary
16 fresh sea scallops (about 1¼ pounds)
Kosher salt
3 bell peppers, ideally one each of red,
green, and yellow, cut into 1-inch pieces

1. Put the lemon juice in a bowl and whisk in the olive oil. Stir in the garlic and rosemary and set aside.

2. Preheat a grill to medium-low heat.

3. Meanwhile, season the scallops on the top and bottom with salt. Skewer one piece of bell pepper onto a large metal or presoaked bamboo skewer. Follow it with a scallop, skewering through either side. Add another pepper, one more scallop, and end with a pepper. Repeat with the remaining 7 skewers and the remaining scallops and peppers.

4. Brush the skewers with some of the lemon marinade. Add to the grill and cook, turning once very carefully, until grill marks appear on both sides and the center of the scallops look opaque and white, 8 to 10 minutes. Remove and brush with more marinade if desired.

5. Divide the skewers among individual plates, or present family style from a platter, and serve warm.

ROASTED & GRILLED BABY BACK PORK RIBS

{ SERVES 4 }

Whenever my dad roasted pork ribs back in the day, the best part was the leftovers, which he'd throw on the grill, adding smoky flavor to the succulent pork. The next-day ribs were so much better that, today, I never wait for the leftover part; instead, I roast the ribs and grill them right away.

This recipe is designed to be served as part of a spread, with three or four ribs per person. To serve it as an entrée, or to serve more people as part of a spread, simply double the recipe.

2 tablespoons paprika
2½ teaspoons kosher salt
¼ teaspoon cayenne pepper
1 teaspoon freshly ground black pepper
½ teaspoon ground mustard
1 rack baby back pork ribs, about 3 pounds
Barbecue sauce, for serving

1. Put the paprika, salt, cayenne, black pepper, and mustard in a medium bowl and stir them together.

2. Use a paring knife to start to pull off the membrane on the back of the ribs; finish pulling with your hands until you have removed the membrane; discard it. Cut away any large chunks of fat, which are easy to remove without cutting deeply into the meat. Season the ribs with the spice mixture, starting on the meaty side and rubbing until evenly coated all over. Set on a large plate or platter and refrigerate for 1 hour.

3. When ready to cook and serve the ribs, preheat the oven to 325°F. Put the ribs on a rack or large broiling pan set over a roasting pan or rimmed baking sheet; roast, meat-side up, until some of the fat renders and the top is slightly crispy, about 1 hour 15 minutes.

4. Remove the ribs from the oven and, when cool enough to handle, wrap carefully in aluminum foil. Clean the drippings from the pan, or use a clean pan, and place the ribs directly on the pan. Roast again until falling-apart tender, about 2 hours. Remove the ribs from the pan and let rest until ready to grill. (Ribs can be refrigerated in an airtight container for a few hours or up to 1 day and reheated on the grill.)

5. Preheat a grill to medium heat. Add the ribs meat-side down to the grill and cook, checking to be sure they're not darkening too quickly, until the meat is heated through and the outside is nicely charred and crusty, about 10 minutes. Transfer the ribs to a cutting board, baste with barbecue sauce, cut between the ribs to separate them, and serve, or serve with the sauce for dipping.

SHORTCAKES WITH GRILLED PEACHES & MASCARPONE

{ SERVES 6 }

We created this peach-centered version of strawberry shortcake late one summer when we took the kids on a tour of New Jersey farms and farm stands and came home with an unbelievable amount of insanely juicy peaches. The mascarpone in place of whipped cream came about out of necessity—the night we made these, we were out of whipped cream!

Vegetable oil, for brushing

3 firm-ripe peaches, pitted and cut into ¾-inch-thick slices

6 individual shortcakes, or 6 thick slices pound cake

1 cup mascarpone

1 tablespoon honey

½ teaspoon pure vanilla extract

1 to 2 tablespoons heavy cream or half-and-half

Sliced almonds, for serving

Fresh mint for serving, optional

1. Preheat a grill to medium heat. Brush the grates lightly with oil and grill the peach slices, turning once, until marked on both sides, about 4 minutes total. If desired, grill the shortcake (top side only) or pound cake slices until marks appear, about 1 minute. Transfer the shortcakes or pound cake slices to 6 serving plates and top with the peaches.

2. Put the mascarpone, honey, vanilla extract, and cream in a small bowl, and stir together briefly. Dollop over the peaches and short-cakes. Garnish with the sliced almonds and fresh mint leaves, if desired, and serve.

MEMORIAL DAY GRILL CAKE

{ MAKES ONE 9-INCH CAKE }

This is a go-for-broke theme cake like a smaller version of something we might make on *Cake Boss*. For my money, Memorial Day isn't just the unofficial first day of summer; it's also the first day of what I think of as the "grilling season," so here's an edible grill, with the grate made out of fondant, as well as a steak, hot dogs, and hamburgers—the works! When making the meats for this cake, the color of the combined fondant doesn't have to be exactly what's pictured here; you can go redder for less well-done meat if that's the way you like it, or browner if you like your meat more well done.

If you own a clay gun, you can use it to make the grill grates rather than rolling out such long coils.

Two 9-inch cakes of your choosing (pages 292 to 298), filled with your choice of filling (pages 302 to 311)

4 cups white Decorator's Buttercream (page 302) in a pastry bag fitted with #6 star tip

About 2 pounds black fondant

1 pound gray fondant (14 ounces white fondant and 2 ounces black fondant, kneaded together)

About 9 ounces meat-colored fondant (about 4 ounces each of red and brown fondant, with about 1 ounce of white, kneaded together)

Small piece white fondant

Brown food coloring or gel

Small piece cheese-colored fondant (about 2 ounces of yellow fondant with a pinch of red fondant kneaded in)

TOOLS & EQUIPMENT

X-ACTO knife or sharp, thin-bladed knife such as a paring knife

Water pen

Paintbrush

2½-inch round cookie cutter

Fondant ribbon cutter

Fondant smoother

Steamer

1. On a turntable, prepare a double-layer cake on a doily-lined cardboard circle, and dirty-ice it without the tip (page 287). Drape the cake with black fondant, smooth it in place with the smoother, and trim it (page 289). Do not return unused fondant to its container; you will need it to make a band at the end. Steam the cake with the steamer (a).

2. Roll the gray fondant into a coil with a ¼-inch diameter (b).

3. Lay the coil across the center of the top of the cake (c). Trim the ends with the X-ACTO knife at a slight angle to make it easier to lay the perimeter of the grate alongside it.

4. Lay another piece of coil across the first one, forming a cross in the center of the cake; trim the ends of the coil at a slight angle to make it easier to lay the perimeter of the grate alongside it.

5. Lay additional pieces of coil across the cake ½ inch apart (d), then wrap a piece of coil around the perimeter of the cake, trim it to fit, and press it into place (e).

6. Shape the meat-colored fondant into a piece of steak. Make a small "T" out of white fondant, representing bone (f), and apply it to the steak with a water pen.

7. Press a brush or other implement into the steak to make "grill marks" (g), then paint the meat with food coloring (h) and place it on the grill (i).

j

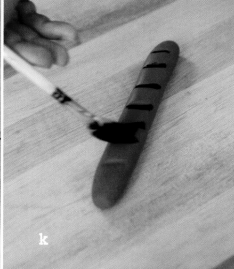

k

l

m

n

o

p

q

r

8. Roll out some of the meat-colored fondant to make a hot dog (j). Press a brush or other implement into the hot dog to make "grill marks" and paint the marks with food coloring (k). Place hot dog on grill (l).

9. Make two burgers by shaping the remaining meat-colored fondant into a half-inch-thick piece and punching two 2½-inch circles out with a cutter. Add texture by patting the patties with a kitchen towel (m) and pressing a brush or other implement into the burgers to make "grill marks" (n). Place burgers on grill (o).

10. Make two pieces of cheese (p) by rolling the yellow fondant out to ⅛-inch thick and cutting two 2½-inch squares out of it with the X-ACTO knife (use a ruler or other straight edge to guide you). Use a water pen to affix the cheese to the burgers, ruffling the edges to simulate a "melting" effect (q, r).

11. Steam the top of the cake.

12. Add a band around the base of the cake: Use a strip cutter to cut a 1-inch band out of the black fondant. Steam the side of the cake and affix the band to the cake.

MANLY MAN FATHER'S DAY FEAST

Father's Day has always been a very special holiday for me, not only because I enjoy celebrating with Lisa and our kids, but also because it gives me a chance to reflect on what a great dad my own father was, and to spend a little time evaluating how I stack up against his example. Every year, I think the same thing: that I'll always be striving to live up to his incredible standards, although I may never quite get there. Of course, my own kids don't look it that way: On Father's Day, they make me feel like the best dad in the world, bringing me their hand-made cards first thing in the morning, then joining me for the break-fast that Lisa makes—scrambled eggs, muffins, bacon, sausage, pancakes, and coffee—that is a feast fit for a king. We don't see the rest of the family on Father's Day; I just want to be with my immediate family and soak up everything each of them has to offer. But I do sometimes get together with my best pals and fellow fathers around Father's Day for a little celebration of our own. For that guys' dinner, we indulge in steak and potatoes, and the side dishes and desserts that go along with them. Here are some of my favorites, including a few inspired by my own childhood memories and my own kids; what could be more appropriate for Father's Day?

ROASTED RIB EYES WITH HORSERADISH BUTTER

{ SERVES 4 }

Shown here with Sesame Green Beans, recipe on page 144.

Of course, the centerpiece of any Father's Day Feast has to be steak, and these rib eyes don't disappont; the horseradish butter offers peppery relief to the fatty decadence of the beef.

Four ¾- to 1-inch-thick boneless rib eye
   steaks (about 2½ pounds total), excess
   fat trimmed
Kosher salt
Freshly ground black pepper
Olive oil
1 tablespoon unsalted butter,
   room temperature
½ teaspoon prepared horseradish,
   or to taste
1 teaspoon Dijon mustard

1. Pat the steaks dry and set them out at room temperature 30 minutes to an hour before cooking. Meanwhile, position a rack in the top third of the oven and preheat the oven to 450°F.

2. Working on a rimmed baking sheet, season the steaks generously with salt and pepper, then rub each with a light coating of olive oil. Roast until the steaks are browned on top and feel springy to the touch in the center, 7 to 8 minutes for medium rare, or 9 to 10 minutes for medium.

3. Meanwhile, in a small bowl, mash together the softened butter, horseradish, and mustard. Season with a pinch each of salt and pepper. Transfer the steaks to 4 plates and dollop or spread each with some of the horseradish butter. Serve warm.

SESAME GREEN BEANS

{ SERVES 4 TO 6 }
Photograph on page 142.

When I was a kid and my parents took me and my sisters out for the occasional Chinese dinner in Hoboken, one of my favorite dishes was always sesame green beans; I especially loved it alongside sliced beef dishes such as beef with bamboo shoots or beef and broccoli. To this day, when I have a steak at home, one of my favorite things to cook it with is these sesame green beans.

1½ pounds green beans, ends trimmed
1 tablespoon sesame seeds, optional
2 tablespoons olive oil
1 teaspoon dark sesame oil, optional
Kosher salt
Freshly ground black pepper

1. Fill a large, lidded pot with about ½-inch water. Add the green beans, cover the pot, and bring the water to a simmer over medium-high heat. Let cook until the beans become bright green and crisp-tender, 4 to 5 minutes. Drain in a colander and rinse with cold running water; let drain, then pat dry thoroughly with paper towels. (Drying the beans off is important so the green beans won't splatter later when you put them in the hot pan.)

2. In a large, deep skillet over medium-low heat, toast the sesame seeds until lightly browned and fragrant, about 4 minutes, shaking the pan to prevent scorching. Remove the pan from the heat, drizzle in the olive oil and the sesame oil (if using), then add the green beans. Return the pan back to the heat and toss the beans quickly and thoroughly with tongs to re-warm them and coat them in the seeds and oil. Let cook until the beans are warmed through, 1 to 2 minutes. Season generously with salt and pepper, transfer to a serving bowl, and serve warm.

ICEBERG WEDGES WITH BLUE CHEESE DRESSING & BACON

{ SERVES 4 TO 6 }

If there's such a thing as a meaty salad, this is it: wedges of iceberg lettuce with rich, creamy blue cheese dressing, and bits of bacon. This is the perfect starter to go with any meat-based dinner, especially steak.

4 to 6 slices bacon
½ cup mayonnaise
2 tablespoons olive oil
¼ cup crumbled blue cheese
Freshly ground black pepper
1 large head iceberg lettuce
¼ red onion, finely chopped
¾ cup fresh cherry tomatoes, halved lengthwise

1. In a large skillet over medium heat, lay the whole bacon pieces side by side (slightly overlapping or wrinkled is fine). Cook, using tongs to turn occasionally, until browned and crispy, about 8 to 10 minutes. Use the tongs to transfer the slices to a paper-towel–lined plate to drain.

2. Meanwhile, put the mayonnaise in a small bowl. Whisk in the olive oil one tablespoon at a time, until the mixture is smooth and creamy. Stir in 2 heaping tablespoons of the blue cheese. Season with black pepper and set aside.

3. Trim the woody base off the lettuce head and remove any browned or wilted leaves of lettuce. Cut the head into 4 or 6 equal wedges, being sure each contains some of the core to hold it together.

4. Set 1 lettuce wedge on each of 4 to 6 plates. Drizzle with some of the blue cheese dressing. Top with the remaining crumbled blue cheese and the chopped red onions. Using your fingers, crumble the bacon pieces over the top of the wedges. Garnish the plates with the cherry tomatoes and serve.

TWICE-BAKED POTATOES

{ MAKES 4 }

Lisa makes a version of this recipe at home, and it's a potato lover's dream come true, combining mashed potatoes and baked potatoes in one side dish: You bake the potatoes, then remove the flesh, mash or mill it, and return it to the skins. They're a little more work than most potato dishes, but worth every second of effort.

4 large russet (Idaho) potatoes,
  scrubbed clean
4 tablespoons unsalted butter, melted
Kosher salt
Freshly ground black pepper
½ cup sour cream
1 tablespoon chopped fresh flat-leaf parsley
  or chopped chives

1. Position a rack in the center of the oven and preheat the oven to 425°F. Rub the potato skins with some of the melted butter (about 2 tablespoons), and season all over with salt and pepper. Transfer to a rimmed baking sheet or roasting pan and bake until very tender when pierced with a paring knife, about 50 minutes. Remove from the oven and let cool slightly.

2. When the potatoes are cool enough to handle, cut a hole into the long side of each, leaving a thin border on all sides. Using a spoon, carefully scoop out the flesh from the center of the potato and place it in a bowl. Either transfer the flesh to a ricer, or mash it thoroughly with a fork or potato masher until smooth. Combine the mashed potato with the sour cream, the remaining melted butter, and season with salt and pepper. Pipe or spoon the potato mixture back into the potato holes. (At this point, you can refrigerate the potatoes in an airtight container for up to 1 day. Let come to room temperature before baking again.)

3. Transfer the potatoes to the oven and bake again until the centers are warm and the tops are lightly browned, about 20 minutes. Serve, garnished with parsley or chives.

CHOCOLATE PEANUT BUTTER ICEBOX CAKE

{ SERVES 6 }

My son Buddy has always had a thing for Reese's peanut butter cups. He loves them so much he could do a commercial for them. For his birthday one year, I came up with this chocolate and peanut butter dessert. It came out so good that it became one of *my* favorites as well. It's a great dish for entertaining because it's easy to make, doesn't require baking, and keeps well in the refrigerator.

½ cup creamy peanut butter
¼ cup brown sugar
¼ teaspoon pure vanilla extract
⅛ teaspoon kosher salt
2 cups heavy cream
One box (9 ounces) chocolate wafer cookies
2 tablespoons chopped roasted peanuts

1. Put the peanut butter, brown sugar, vanilla, and salt in a large bowl and whisk together.

2. Using an electric mixer, whip the cream until stiff peaks form, about 3 minutes (try not to overmix, or the mixture will become grainy). Use a spatula to fold the cream into the peanut butter until no streaks remain.

3. Dab the bottom of 6 chocolate wafers with a scant amount of the cream mixture to help them stay in place. Set them on a large serving platter to form a filled-in circle (one in the middle, and 5 around its perimeter). Add about one cup of the peanut butter-cream mixture in the center, and spread slightly leaving just a small edge of the cookies showing. Repeat to make 4 layers, ending with a cream layer (you should have four layers each of cookies and cream). Sprinkle the cake with the peanuts.

4. Store in the refrigerator at least 2 hours or overnight. To serve, slice into wedges.

STOUT FLOATS

{ MAKES 4 }

We're not an Irish family, but we get into the Saint Patrick's Day spirit when the holiday rolls around every year: The counter staff all wear green, and we offer green cupcakes and cannoli filled with green cream. One year, after we closed the shop, my brother in-law Mauro impro-vised this adult version of a root beer float for Saint Patrick's Day. Ever since then, whenever I throw a guys' get together, these are one of the favorite desserts.

For a kid-friendly version, replace the stout with root beer.

About 45 ounces stout beer, such as
    Guinness (about 3 large cans)
1 pint vanilla ice cream
Freshly grated nutmeg, for dusting (optional)

Fill 4 float glasses or juice glasses with ½ cup each (about 2 scoops) of the ice cream. Top slowly with stout. (You may not use all of the stout.) Garnish with nutmeg, if desired. Serve the floats with a spoon.

FATHER'S DAY BEER CAKE

{ MAKES ONE 13 BY 9-INCH CAKE }

Whether or not you serve this cake with the menu of dishes in this chapter, it's still the perfect way to celebrate Dad, with a beer and pretzel theme (set against a hardwood floor) that makes you think of men, summer, watching a ballgame, and kicking back. Mix the fondant beer color to resemble Dad's favorite brew: darker for stouts and Guinness-style, blonder for pale ale or pilsner style, and so on.

13 by 9 by 2-inch cake of your choosing (pages 292 to 298), cut in half to make two 6½ by 9-inch layers, filled with your choice of filling (pages 302 to 311)

4 cups white Decorator's Buttercream (page 302) in a pastry bag fitted with #6 interchangeable plain tip

24 ounces white fondant

6 ounces brown fondant

1 pound beer-colored fondant (brown, yellow, and white kneaded together to form the color beer desired, (see headnote)

About 6 ounces pretzel-colored fondant (3 ounces each of ivory and brown, kneaded together)

1 tablespoon crystal sugar

About 6 ounces blue fondant

TOOLS & EQUIPMENT
Fondant smoother

Strip cutter

X-ACTO knife, or other sharp, thin-bladed knife, such as a paring knife

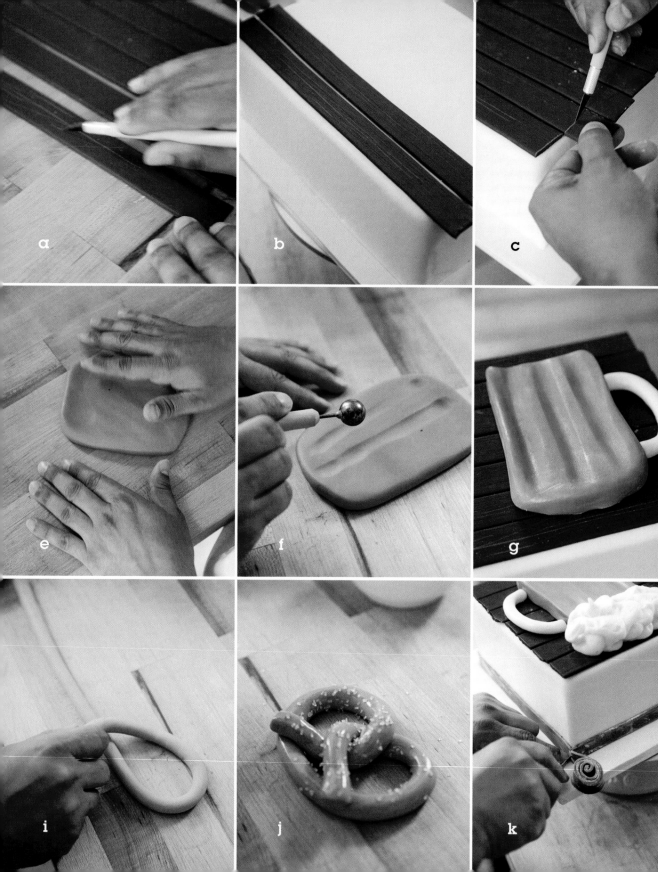

1. On a turntable, prepare a double-layer rectangular cake on a doily-lined cardboard rectangle, filling it with the filling of your choice and dirty-icing it without the tip (page 287). Drape the cake with white fondant, smooth it in place with the smoother, and trim it (page 289).

2. Roll the brown fondant out to a rectangle, ⅛-inch thick and at least 13 inches by 7 inches. Cut seven 1-inch-wide strips with a strip cutter. Use the back of the X-ACTO knife to score the strips lengthwise to mimic the grain of a wood floor (a).

3. Steam the cake and lay the floor pieces across the top of the cake (b), trimming them with the X-ACTO knife so they just cover the top of the cake (c).

4. Roll out the beer-colored fondant to ½-inch thick (d), and shape into a rounded rectangle (e). Make 3 vertical ridges using the back of a melon baller to mimic the ridges on a glass (f).

5. Fashion a handle with white fondant. Affix the mug and handle to the cake with buttercream (g). Pipe buttercream on top of the mug to imitate the foam over a mug of beer (h).

6. Roll the pretzel-colored fondant out into a coil about ½-inch in diameter. Shape it into a pretzel (i). Top with crystal sugar (to imitate salt), and apply to the cake with buttercream (j).

7. Roll the blue fondant out ⅛-inch thick and at least 1-inch wide by 40-inches long. Cut two ¾-inch strips with a strip cutter. Roll them into 2 coils. Steam the cake and unspool one strip around the cake, starting at the base to make a border (k). Add the last coil around the top, allowing the edge to go about ⅛-inch above the cake to cover the ends of the floor pieces to make a neat border (l).

8. Steam the cake around the sides to make the border shiny.

FOURTH OF JULY

All Americans are proud of their country, but coming as I do from a family of immigrants—both my father and my mother were born in Italy—I have that extra appreciation passed down directly from people who came here and found the dream promised to one and all by this great country. We always take time out to celebrate the Fourth of July, usually by getting together for a pool party. The dishes here are a tribute to some favorite summertime foods, with our patriotism really showing through in the desserts we serve: red-white-and-blue strawberries, and a spectacular American flag cake made with berries that commemorate summer's bounty and America's birthday at the same time.

CHILI CON QUESO

{ SERVES 6 TO 8 }

The slightly spicy, deliciously thick, and creamy cheese dip isn't nearly as American as apple pie, but when friends get together for a summer celebration, it often seems the perfect way to kick things off.

1 tablespoon unsalted butter
½ small yellow onion, finely diced
1 can (4.5 ounces) chopped green chiles
1 tablespoon all-purpose flour
2 cups shredded jack or Mexican cheese mix
2½ cups shredded orange Cheddar cheese
½ cup tomato salsa
½ cup sour cream
½ cup milk or water
Finely grated zest of 1 lime
Kosher salt
Freshly ground black pepper
Chopped cilantro, for garnish
Tortilla chips, for serving

1. Melt the butter in a medium, heavy saucepan over medium heat. Add the onion and cook, stirring, until softened but not browned, 4 to 5 minutes. Add the chiles, then stir in the flour until well combined.

2. Add the cheese in two batches, stirring until mostly melted between additions. Stir in the salsa, sour cream, milk or water, and lime zest; cook, stirring occasionally, until smooth and gently bubbling. Season with salt and pepper to taste. Garnish with the cilantro. Serve warm straight from the pot or in a warmed ceramic bowl with the tortilla chips.

FLANK STEAK WITH ITALIAN SALSA VERDE

{ SERVES 4 TO 6 }

Shown here with Black-eyed Peas Salad, recipe on page 162.

We Valastros love our American home, and we love our Italian heritage just as much. So, for a lot of holidays, we combine the two. This is a great example: A grilled steak is about as American as you can get and the *salsa verde* is a traditional Italian condiment for grilled meats, especially with the assortment called *grigliata mista*, or mixed grill.

1½ to 2 pounds flank steak
Kosher salt
Freshly ground black pepper
1½ cups chopped flat-leaf parsley
    (about ½ bunch)
Leaves from 6 to 8 sprigs fresh oregano
    (about ¼ cup)
2 large cloves garlic
1 tablespoon freshly squeezed lemon juice
    plus finely grated zest of 1 lemon
    (2 teaspoons)
¼ cup olive oil
3 anchovies in oil, coarsely chopped
    (optional)

1. Season the steak with salt and pepper and let sit at room temperature 30 minutes before grilling. Meanwhile, preheat the grill to medium-high heat.

2. Grill the steak over direct heat, turning once, 6 to 8 minutes per side for medium-rare, a bit longer for more well done. Remove and transfer to a platter or cutting board; tent loosely with aluminum foil and let rest 5 to 10 minutes.

3. Meanwhile, make the *salsa verde*: Put the parsley, oregano, garlic, lemon juice and zest, olive oil, and anchovies (if using) in a food processor. Pulse until well-chopped, about 30 seconds. Slice the flank steak thinly against the grain, arrange on plates or a platter, and dollop with the *salsa verde*.

BLACK-EYED PEAS SALAD

{ SERVES 4 }

Photograph on page 160.

This is a great American story for a Fourth of July Dish: I had never had black-eyed peas until a little girl from Georgia moved to New Jersey with her family and ended up at our kids' school. Lisa invited them to our Fourth of July party one year, and they brought a version of this dish to the buffet. Ever since then, we've been serving it as part of our own roster of dishes.

2 cans (15.5-ounces each) black-eyed peas, drained
6 tablespoons crumbled feta cheese
2 teaspoons sherry vinegar or red wine vinegar
½ cup grape tomatoes, quartered
Pinch of kosher salt and freshly ground black pepper
⅓ cup loosely packed fresh flat-leaf parsley
¼ teaspoon crushed red-pepper flakes (optional)

Combine all the ingredients in a serving bowl, and toss well. Let stand 10 minutes before serving.

GRILLED CHILI-LIME SHRIMP SKEWERS

{ SERVES 4 }

My favorite summertime drink is an ice-cold beer and Lisa's is a margarita. When we host a poolside party, these skewers are almost always on the menu because they go so well with both.

½ cup honey
1 lime, halved
1 tablespoon Asian chili paste, or to taste
24 large raw shrimp (about 1 pound), peeled and deveined
Kosher salt

1. Put the honey, juice of ½ lime, and chili paste in a bowl, and whisk until combined.

2. Preheat a grill or grill pan to medium-high heat. Season the shrimp with salt and skewer 6 at a time onto metal or pre-soaked wooden skewers. Brush the shrimp with some of the honey-chili mixture. Grill, turning once, until lightly marked and opaque on the inside, 3 to 4 minutes per side. Transfer to a serving platter and squeeze with the juice from the other half of the lime.

PLUM GALETTE

{ SERVES 8 }

This simple, summery tart showcases one of the telltale fruits of the season, which also happens to be a favorite of my son Marco.

1¼ cups all-purpose flour

3 tablespoons plus ½ teaspoon granulated sugar

Kosher salt

1 stick (½ cup) unsalted butter, cut into small pieces and well chilled

¼ cup ice-cold water, plus more if needed

5 to 6 large firm, ripe plums

1½ teaspoons tapioca starch, plus more for dusting

Finely grated zest of ½ lemon

2 tablespoons heavy cream

Vanilla ice cream, for serving (optional)

1. Put the flour, 1 tablespoon of the sugar, and ½ teaspoon of salt in the bowl of a food processor and pulse to combine. Add the butter and pulse just until the mixture resembles a coarse meal. Stream in the ice water and pulse again to incorporate. Pinch the dough with your fingers to test; it should hold together without being sticky. Turn it out onto a piece of plastic wrap and form into a disk. Refrigerate until firm, about 1 hour.

2. A few minutes before the dough is ready, slice the plums into ½-inch-thick pieces. Put 2 tablespoons of the granulated sugar, the tapioca starch, a pinch of salt, and the lemon zest in a large bowl. Gently toss the plums in the sugar mixture to coat. Transfer the plums to a strainer and set the strainer over the bowl to catch any juices that run out. Reserve the juices.

3. Position a rack in the center of the oven and preheat the oven to 375°F. Roll out the dough into a ¼-inch-thick disk and transfer to a parchment- or silicone-mat–lined baking sheet. Very lightly dust the bottom of the crust with more tapioca starch. Start laying the plum slices on their sides in a circular pattern with their edges touching or slightly overlapping; leave about a 1½-inch border around the edge of the dough. Continue lining the inside of the circle with more plums until the surface is covered. Fold the edges of the dough around the plums, folding and pinching the dough as needed.

4. Brush the outer edges of the dough with cream. Sprinkle the top of the plums and the edge of the dough with ½ teaspoon more sugar.

5. Bake until the crust is lightly browned and the juices of the plums are sizzling, about 45 minutes. If the plums look dry when you remove the tart, brush the fruit with a very small amount of the reserved juices. Let cool. Serve sliced into wedges with the ice cream, if desired

RED, WHITE & BLUE STRAWBERRIES

{ MAKES 12 }

America's birthday calls for red-white-and-blue desserts and this is an easy one to make ahead of time, although they should be eaten on the same day they're prepared so that they don't become soft or soggy. You can even serve these before or alongside a more substantial dessert, such as the Fourth of July Flag Cake on page 171.

8 ounces (2 bars) good-quality
    white chocolate, coarsely chopped
Pinch of kosher salt
¼ cup blue decorating sugar or sprinkles
12 large strawberries, with their stems

1. Put the chocolate in a heatproof bowl and set it over a pot of simmering water (do not let the bowl touch the water); cook, stirring frequently with a rubber spatula, until melted. Stir in a pinch of salt. Remove from the stove.

2. Put the sugar in a small bowl. Line a baking sheet with parchment or wax paper. One by one, dip the berries two-thirds of the way into the melted chocolate to coat. Then dip the tips (about ⅓ of the berries) into the sugar or sprinkles. Transfer to the prepared baking sheet and refrigerate until set, at least 1 hour. Serve cold.

FOURTH OF JULY FLAG CAKE

{ MAKES ONE 13 BY 9-INCH CAKE }

For me, this is the ultimate summertime cake: It's obviously perfect for Independence Day because of its flag design, but it's also a showcase for blueberries and raspberries, both of which are at their peak during mid- to late summer. Basically, this is an revved-up berry shortcake and it's perfect for any large summertime gathering.

As with any cake, you can use whatever type of batter you like, but I urge you to make this with vanilla to let the flavor of the berries and cream really shine.

Two 13 by 9-inch cakes of your choosing
(pages 292 to 298)
About 10 cups Italian Whipped Cream
(page 311) or other whipped cream in a
pastry bag fitted with #6 star tip
12 large fresh strawberries, 4 thinly sliced,
8 halved
About 1½ cups fresh blueberries
About 2 pints fresh raspberries

a

b

d

e

1. On a turntable, prepare a rectangular cake on a doily-lined cardboard rectangle. Pipe whipped cream over the top of the cake, first along the sides, then filling in the center (a).

2. Scatter the sliced strawberries over the cream (b), top with the second cake, and ice as you did the first layer (c).

3. Ice the entire cake with whipped cream (d). (While you can usually smooth the sides of a cake with a cake spatula or comb [page 286], I recommend a comb here because it makes the cake seem more regal, like a flag.)

4. Create the stars on the flag by making a rectangle with blueberries, 4 inches long and 5 inches wide. Fill in the rectangle with blueberries and press down gently with an open palm to make them even. Create 7 stripes out of the raspberries, making sure that they border the cake at the top and bottom (e). (Tip: To be sure the stripes are evenly spaced, mark their left margin with 1 raspberry before filling them in.)

5. Pipe swirly dabs of whipped cream at 1-inch intervals around the base of the cake, and set a halved strawberry between each dab (f).

FALL TAILGATE

Watching football is one of my absolute favorite pastimes. When I was a kid, I used to love hanging with my Dad on a Sunday afternoon, watching a game on television. To me, the sound of an announcer on the tube and the crowds cheering in the background conjure up the spirit of the fall. My dad hasn't been with us for years, but I still love football. As a young man, I began watching with my buds, and today, I unplug from the rest of the world and lounge around my house in a Giants jersey, and let the game wash over me. Sometimes family or friends will come over, but only those who know that the game rules the day and, if we're lucky, Lisa might cook up some snacks for us. Of course, the ultimate fan experience isn't in the living room, but in the sports stadium, with a tailgate party before you head in, claim your seats, and cheer until your voice goes hoarse. This chapter features some of my favorite tailgate foods, the kind of hearty, big-flavored grub you crave at a sporting event. When I head out to the ball field, I always bring a grill along, and a few of the recipes ahead assume that you do the same.

CAYENNE PEANUTS

{ MAKES 2 CUPS, SERVING 6 TO 8 }

You know that old song, "Take Me Out to the Ballgame," and the line, "Buy me some peanuts and Cracker Jack"? Well, my favorite ballpark snack is peanuts, and whenever we throw a tailgate party, I always make my special blend, coating them with my own mixture of sugar, salt, and spices. It's an addictively sweet and spicy mix that's become an in-demand spectator snack for my entire extended family; sometimes my relatives will ask me to whip up a bag even if I'm not joining them to watch the game!

The cayenne adds heat, so if that's not your thing, leave it out, or use a little less.

1 tablespoon unsalted butter
2 cups roasted unsalted peanuts
2 teaspoons granulated sugar
1½ teaspoons cayenne pepper
1½ teaspoons ground paprika
1 teaspoon ground coriander seed
½ teaspoon kosher salt

1. Position a rack in the center of the oven and preheat the oven to 350°F. Line a rimmed baking sheet with foil.

2. Set a small, heavy saucepan over low heat, add the butter, and melt it. Add the peanuts and toss to coat. Stir in the sugar, cayenne pepper, paprika, coriander, and salt.

3. Spread the nuts out onto the prepared baking sheet in a single layer. Roast until crispy and fragrant, 6 to 8 minutes, shaking the pan occasionally to ensure even cooking and keep the nuts from scorching.

4. Remove the sheet from the oven and let the nuts cool. Serve immediately or store in a sealed container or bag at room temperature until game day, but no longer than 2 days.

SPINACH-ARTICHOKE DIP WITH PARMESAN

{ SERVES 4 TO 6 }

This creamy hors d'oeuvre is sinfully rich, bound with a mixture of mayonnaise and Parmesan. It's based on something my mother used to set out when she and my father entertained: a spinach and artichoke dip that she served in a hollowed out peasant bread with crackers alongside for scooping. My version is modernized with tortilla chips, an especially tailgate-appropriate choice, for dipping.

2 cans (14 ounces each) artichoke hearts, drained and squeezed of excess moisture

½ cup frozen thawed spinach, squeezed of excess moisture

1 cup mayonnaise (regular or reduced fat)

½ cup finely grated Parmesan

1 can (4.5 ounces) green chilies, drained

Freshly ground black pepper

Tortilla chips

1. Position a rack in the center of the oven and preheat the oven to 375°F.

2. Finely chop the artichoke hearts and spinach and squeeze out any extra juices that develop. Transfer them to a large bowl. Add the mayonnaise, Parmesan, and chilies. Season with pepper, and stir well.

3. Transfer the dip to a 9-inch-square glass baking dish or pie plate. Bake until the top is browned and the dip is cooked through, 35 to 40 minutes.

4. Serve warm or at room temperature, with tortilla chips.

ASIAN PORK SLIDERS

{ MAKES 8 }

My family's go-to Chinese restaurant is Hong Kong Kitchen in East Hanover, New Jersey. We order dinner from there at least once a week. I never get tired of the way Asian flavors pop on the palate, especially soy sauce and ginger, which deliver huge hits of salt and spice. These pork sliders present those elements in a fun way that's just right for a fall afternoon spent watching a ballgame.

To build these, top them with the cole slaw on page 182 (a traditional accompaniment in barbecued pork sandwiches). You can also top them with sliced cucumbers and/or cilantro.

1 pound ground pork
1 tablespoon soy sauce
2 tablespoons minced red onion
½ teaspoon finely grated fresh ginger
8 slider buns or mini potato rolls

1. Preheat a grill to medium heat.

2. Put the pork, soy sauce, red onion, and ginger in a large bowl and stir together to incorporate. Form 8 patties, using 3 to 4 tablespoons of pork mixture in each one and shaping them ½-inch thick. Be sure not to overwork or overhandle the mixture.

3. Grill the burgers over direct heat, turning once, until fully cooked through, 5 to 7 minutes per side.

4. Toward the end of the sliders' grilling time, grill the buns: Slice them in half if necessary, then grill the cut sides until lightly marked and lightly toasted, about 1 minute.

5. Let the sliders rest on a platter or cutting board for 5 minutes after grilling, then set 1 slider in each bun and serve.

TRI-COLORE ASIAN SLAW

{ SERVES 4 TO 6 AS A SIDE }
Enough to top 8 sliders, with a little extra.

Cole slaw belongs to summer for me; You know those days when you reach into the fridge and make a meal out of those cold, refreshing things kept in plastic containers and white butcher paper: cole slaw, potato salad, and deli meats. Yum!

That feeling is part of why we love tailgate parties: They give us a little burst of the outdoors and the carefree spirit of summer, even though we might be eating the food and watching the game in the fall (or winter) and maybe even indoors.

This is a global cole slaw with an Italian name (*tri-colore* means "three color," a nod to the carrots in the cabbage mix), and slightly Asian character thanks to the lime juice and cilantro. It's good on top of the sliders on page 181, or on its own as a side dish to any type of sandwich. You can also serve it with fancier fare like grilled or roasted fish or pork.

6 cups (one 14-ounce bag) cole slaw mix
    with carrot
3 tablespoons freshly squeezed lime juice
3 tablespoons olive oil
2 tablespoons mayonnaise
¼ teaspoon kosher salt
½ teaspoons granulated sugar
1 jalapeño pepper, seeded if desired,
    then thinly sliced
½ cup fresh cilantro leaves, roughly torn

Put all ingredients in a bowl and toss well. Let the slaw sit at least 15 minutes before serving.

SPORTY SUGAR COOKIES

{ MAKES 8 TO 10 FOOTBALL COOKIES; 10 TO 12 ROUND COOKIES }

Sometimes, less is more. When you throw a true tailgate party, outside the gates of a sports venue, or even a potluck get-together at a friend's house, convenience and portability are crucial: For the dessert, you want something that can be made in advance, easily transported to the stadium or party location, and isn't sensitive to heat or cold.

Cookies are the perfect answer to all those needs, and these cookies—made to mimic the look of different sports balls—set the perfect mood as you wrap up your tailgate meal and head to your seats to watch the game.

This chapter is mostly about the fall, but I've included instructions for making baseball, basketball, and tennis cookies as well, so you can have cookies for your favorite sports all year long.

Notes:

The amounts of buttercream and fondant below assume that you are making just one type of cookie—football, baseball, basketball, or tennis ball. If you are making a variety of types, adjust amounts accordingly: you will need approximately 2 tablespoons of buttercream and 1¼ ounce of fondant for decorating each cookie (i.e., in addition to the amount used to affix the fondant to the cookie).

Because these don't use a lot of buttercream, if you'd rather not make your own, it's fine to use prepared icing that comes in little tubes in the supermarket.

Because the white decorator's buttercream used to affix the fondant to the cookie will be spread out, you can use almost any tip to pipe it onto the cookie; a #4 plain tip is called for, below, but if you need that tip for another icing, you can use another tip (such as a #5 tip) instead. For the football cookies, which call for interchangeable tips, pipe the buttercream onto the cookie with no tip attached (just be careful not to use an ex-

cessive amount) or apply the first interchangeable tip for decorating and use that.

For cookies that call for white and another color buttercream, put the necessary amount of white buttercream in a pastry bag first, then color the remaining buttercream as necessary.

Sugar cookies (recipe follows), baked in desired shapes

FOOTBALL COOKIES:

About 1 pound dark chocolate fondant
About 2 cups white Decorator's Buttercream
(page 302) in a pastry bag fitted with
a coupler
#48 interchangeable basket weave tip
#4 interchangeable plain tip

Roll the fondant out to ⅛ inch. Use the same cutter you used for the cookies to cut the fondant into the same number of footballs/ ovals.

a

b

c

d

e

f

g

h

i

Lay cookies on a flat surface so they won't break as you decorate them. Pipe some buttercream onto the top of each cookie and spread it out with a cake spatula (a). (For football cookies, apply the buttercream using the bag with no tip attached to the coupler; for round cookies, use the #4 tip or another tip; see notes, page 185.) Apply the football-shaped fondant to the cookies (b). Affix the #48 interchangeable basket weave tip to the bag, and with the ruffled side of the tip facing downward toward the cookie, pipe a line across the center of the cookie lengthwise, then a line at the front and back of the cookie to mimic the stitching on a football (c). Change to the #4 plain interchangeable tip to pipe stitching across the center line.

BASKETBALL COOKIES:

About 1 pound orange fondant
About ½ cup white Decorator's Buttercream
    (page 302) in a pastry bag fitted with
    #4 plain tip
About 1 cup brown Decorator's Buttercream
    (page 302) in a pastry bag fitted with
    #4 plain tip

Roll orange fondant out to 1/8-inch thick and punch 3½-inch circles out of it using the same punch you used to make the cookies; affix to cookies with buttercream (see football instructions), and pipe black stitching to mimic a basketball (d, e).

BASEBALL COOKIES:

About 1 pound white fondant
About ½ cup white Decorator's Buttercream
    (page 302) in a pastry bag fitted with
    #4 plain tip
About 1 cup red Decorator's Buttercream
    (page 302) in a pastry bag fitted with
    #4 plain tip

Roll white fondant out to ⅛-inch thick and punch 3½-inch circles out of it using the same punch you used to make the cookies; affix to cookies with buttercream (see football instructions), and pipe red stitching to mimic a baseball (f, g).

TENNIS BALL COOKIES:

About 1 pound lime green fondant
    (knead together 8 ounces each of green
    and yellow fondant)
About 2 cups white Decorator's Buttercream
    (page 302) in a pastry bag fitted with
    #4 plain tip

Roll lime green fondant out to $1/8$-inch thick and punch 3½-inch circles out of it using the same punch you used to make the cookies; affix to cookies with white buttercream (see football instructions), and pipe white stitching to mimic a tennis ball (h, i).

SUGAR COOKIES

{ MAKES 8 TO 10 FOOTBALL COOKIES; 10 TO 12 ROUND COOKIES }

This is a good, everyday recipe for sugar cookies. You can eat them plain, or decorate them for a wide variety of themes and occasions.

1½ sticks unsalted butter, at room
    temperature
1 cup granulated sugar
1 large egg
1 teaspoon pure vanilla extract
2⅓ cups all-purpose flour, plus more
    for rolling
1 teaspoon baking powder
Pinch kosher salt

1. In the bowl of a stand mixer, cream the butter and sugar on medium-high speed until the butter appears light and fluffy. Scrape down the sides of the bowl and add the egg and vanilla extract; beat to incorporate.

2. In a separate bowl, combine the flour, baking powder, and salt. Working in two batches, add the dry ingredients to the butter mixture on low speed and mix until a dough just forms. Turn the dough onto a piece of plastic wrap and shape into a disk; tightly wrap and refrigerate until firm, 1 to 2 hours.

3. Position a rack in the center of the oven and preheat the oven to 375°F. Line 2 baking sheets with parchment paper. On a lightly floured surface, roll out half the dough at a time into a thin disk. Use cookie cutters to cut the cookies into the desired shapes (3½-inch circles for baseballs, basketballs, and tennis balls; a 5-inch-long football or oval cutter for football season). Repeat with the remaining dough half. (Re-roll dough scraps only once.) Transfer the cookies to the prepared baking sheets and place the sheets in the refrigerator for 15 minutes before baking.

4. Bake until cooked through and lightly golden on the edges, 8 to 10 minutes. Transfer to a rack to cool. (If icing or decorating the cookies, wait until they are completely cooled.)

ALL-PURPOSE COCKTAIL PARTY

Every year, once September has come and gone and the mercury has dropped, I can't wait to begin celebrating the season with cocktail parties at my house. There's just something about the fall that makes you want to spend time with friends and family, basking in the holidays and escaping from the cold outside. My family has always loved entertaining. My mother, who actually sometimes plays the role of an entertainer by singing for one and all, was always a natural hostess. These days, Lisa and I love welcoming people into our home. While a sit-down meal has its place, sometimes it's best to keep things nice and loose with selections that are meant to be enjoyed from a buffet or a passed platter, letting everybody eat when and however much they'd like. This chapter features some of my family's favorite go-to entertaining dishes, including Mini Beef Wellingtons and Potato Pancakes with Crème Fraîche and Caviar, all of which add style to any get-together.

MINI BEEF WELLINGTONS

{ MAKES 18 WELLINGTONS }

In the good old days, on those rare occasions when my parents used to take my sisters and me out for a fancy dinner, beef Wellington was my father's go-to dish. I think he loved it because it's a baker's dish, succulent beef filet and juicy sautéed mushrooms layered together, wrapped in puff pastry, and baked. He can't be at our parties anymore, but I always try to serve these miniature beef wellingtons when we entertain to bring a little of his presence and spirit to any family gathering.

2 sheets frozen puff pastry

2 tablespoons vegetable oil

1½ pounds beef tenderloin, cut into eighteen 1-inch cubes

Kosher salt

Freshly ground black pepper

½ tablespoon unsalted butter

½ shallot, minced

2 packages baby bella mushrooms (8 ounces each), ends trimmed, very finely chopped

½ teaspoon Dijon mustard

¼ teaspoon fresh thyme leaves

1. Thaw the puff pastry at room temperature, position a rack in the center of the oven, and preheat the oven to 400°F.

2. Meanwhile, heat a heavy, medium pan over medium-high heat. Add the oil and heat it, then add the beef, season generously with salt and pepper and sear, stirring occasionally, until browned, about 4 minutes total. (Do not fully cook it.)

3. Heat a small, heavy saucepan over medium-high heat. Add the butter and let it melt and turn foamy. Add the shallots and cook, stir- ring with a wooden spoon, until just softened, 1 minute. Add the mushrooms, mustard, and thyme and cook, stirring, until the mushrooms have released their liquid and are cooked through, 10 to 12 minutes. Remove the pan from the heat.

4. Line a baking sheet with parchment paper. Roll out the puff pastry sheets and cut each into 9 squares. Spoon a scant teaspoon of mushroom mixture onto the center of each square and spread to thin. Top with a piece of beef. Using your fingers, stretch the dough around the beef pieces and pinch the edges together to seal. Trim any excess pastry.

5. Transfer the beef bundles, seam-side down, onto the prepared baking sheet. Bake until the pastry is golden brown and puffed, 22 to 24 minutes. Remove and let cool slightly before serving.

CRAB SALAD IN ENDIVE LEAVES

{ SERVES 6 }

Served here with Potato Pancakes with Crème Fraîche & Caviar, recipe on page 196.

Some version of this hors d'oeuvre has been in rotation at our family's pool parties for as long as I can remember. Although I first discovered it as a summertime treat, I've found that it's equally at home at formal dinners and cocktail parties. The creamy, lemony crab salad and crunchy endive get along great, and it's the perfect canapé because it makes its own vessel, so eliminates one of my pet peeves at cocktail parties: When you're left holding on to, or finding a place to ditch, a plate or spoon after you've eaten something.

8 ounces lump crabmeat, free of shell

Finely grated zest of ½ lemon, plus 1 tablespoon lemon juice

3 tablespoons mayonnaise

2 tablespoons finely chopped celery

1 tablespoon finely chopped shallot

Kosher salt

2 heads endive

Ground paprika or cayenne

1. Put the crabmeat, lemon zest and juice, mayonnaise, celery, and shallots in a bowl and fold together until well incorporated. Season to taste with salt.

2. Carefully pull the leaves from the endive. Spoon some crab salad onto the root end of each leaf. Dust lightly with paprika or cayenne pepper, arrange on a large plate or platter, and serve.

POTATO PANCAKES WITH CRÈME FRAÎCHE & CAVIAR

{ MAKES ABOUT 2½ DOZEN }

Photograph on page 195.

My sister Grace is notorious in our family for her lack of kitchen skills, but this is one dish that she actually cooks to perfection. One of her college roommates made potato pancakes in school and taught Grace how to make them. When she served us these for the first time, the rest of us were pleasantly shocked: They alone were almost worth the cost of her tuition!

Traditionally, potato pancakes are served with apple sauce or sour cream for dipping or dunking. Topping these with crème fraîche and caviar turns an everyday treat into something suitable for even a seated dinner party.

½ yellow onion, minced
2 large russet (Idaho) potatoes
Kosher salt
Freshly ground black pepper
⅓ cup plus 2 tablespoons all-purpose flour
2 large eggs
Vegetable oil, for frying
Crème fraîche
Inexpensive black caviar, such as sturgeon
Fresh dill, coarsely chopped

1. Put the onion in a fine-mesh colander. Peel the potatoes and coarsely grate them using the large-hole side of a box grater. Season generously with salt and pepper, and toss. Using a few paper towels or a clean kitchen towel, squeeze out any excess moisture; then transfer the potato and onion to a large bowl.

2. Sprinkle the potato-onion mixture with the flour and toss to coat. In a separate small bowl, beat the eggs and lightly season with salt and pepper. Add the eggs to the potato mixture and toss to coat. Season again with salt and pepper.

3. Preheat a large nonstick skillet or griddle over medium-high heat and add enough vegetable oil to coat the bottom in a thin layer. Working in batches, scoop 2 heaping tablespoons of the batter at a time into the pan, leaving at least 2 inches between scoops. Using the back of the measuring or other spoon, lightly flatten the potato mounds into thin pancakes. Cook, turning once with a spatula, until golden brown on both sides and soft in the center, about 6 minutes total. Add more oil as needed between batches, and reduce heat to medium if the outsides darken before the centers are cooked.

4. Transfer the potato pancakes to paper-towel–lined plates to drain. Serve dolloped with a small amount of crème fraîche, and sprinkle with caviar and dill to taste.

BOURBON PARTY PUNCH

{ SERVES 6 TO 8 }
Photograph on page 199.

This is my favorite party punch, combining iced tea with a variety of citrus juices and bourbon for a complex and refreshing flavor. Using honey rather than sugar to sweeten the tea gives this brew a smooth taste and texture that keeps you coming back for more.

½ cup honey

8 cups hot brewed black tea

6 cups Kentucky bourbon

¼ cup freshly squeezed lemon juice, plus a few lemon wedges and large strips of zest

¼ cup fresh lime juice, plus a few lime wedges and large strips of zest

¼ cup orange juice, plus a few orange wedges and large strips of zest

1. Whisk the honey into the hot tea and set aside to cool completely; chill until cold.

2. Pour the sweetened iced tea into a large punch bowl or pitcher. Stir in the bourbon, and the lemon, lime, and orange juices, wedges, and zests. Stir well to combine. Ladle or pour into ice-filled glasses.

CHOCOLATE TRUFFLES

{ MAKES ABOUT 4 DOZEN }
Served here with Bourbon Party Punch, recipe on page 197.

These intensely flavored chocolate orbs were the first flourless item that we produced at Carlo's Bake Shop. Although we didn't make them with customer allergies in mind, with all of the gluten concerns that have sprung up in recent years, they've proved to be a welcome option for those visitors who can't eat flour, and we've taken to serving them as a universally enjoyable treat at our holiday parties as well.

16 ounces semisweet chocolate, coarsely
    broken or chopped
1 cup heavy cream
¼ teaspoon kosher salt
¼ teaspoon Triple Sec or other
    orange-flavored liqueur, such as Cointreau
¼ teaspoon pure vanilla extract
1 cup unsweetened cocoa powder

1. Line a baking sheet with parchment or wax paper. Set a large heatproof bowl atop a large pot of simmering water or set a double boiler over simmering water. Add the chocolate, cream, and salt to the bowl and cook, stirring frequently with a heatproof spatula or wooden spoon, until the chocolate is fully melted, about 8 minutes.

2. Remove the bowl from the heat and stir in the orange liqueur and vanilla. Set the bowl aside to cool completely, about 1 hour.

3. Put the cocoa powder in a bowl. Using a small cookie scooper or a scant tablespoon measure, spoon balls of the chocolate mixture and form into a perfect ball using your hands, working quickly to keep the chocolate from melting. Roll in the cocoa powder and transfer to the prepared baking sheet. Keep stored in an airtight container.

PASS-AROUND VANILLA CAKES

{ MAKES ABOUT 25, SERVING 12 }

We pass around hors d'oeuvres at cocktail parties, so why not desserts?
These little cakes, with the choice of frosting left up to you, are a useful addition to your repertoire of
go-to desserts because they get along with every occasion and menu.

1 stick unsalted butter, at room temperature,
    plus more for greasing
1½ cups all-purpose flour, plus more
    for dusting
1 cup sugar
2 eggs
2 teaspoons pure vanilla extract
1 teaspoon baking powder
½ teaspoon baking soda
¼ teaspoon kosher salt
½ cup buttermilk
2 cups of your choice of frosting in a
    pastry bag fitted with #6 star tip
Shredded sweetened coconut, toasted
    if desired, for serving

1. Grease the bottom and sides of a 10-inch-square cake pan and line it with parchment paper, neatly folding the paper into the corners. Carefully grease the bottom and sides of the parchment paper, then lightly coat with flour, tapping out any excess. Position a rack in the center of the oven and preheat to 350°F.

2. Put the butter and sugar in the bowl of a stand mixer and cream them at medium-high speed, scraping down the sides of the mixer once or twice, until the butter looks light and fluffy, about 3 minutes. One by one, add the eggs, beating them in completely after each addition and scraping down the sides of the bowl once. Beat in the vanilla.

3. Sift the flour, baking powder, baking soda, and salt into a large bowl. Slowly add about one-third of the dry ingredients to the wet in the mixer on low speed. Add about ⅓ of the buttermilk, and continue alternating with the dry ingredients until both the flour mixture and the buttermilk are just incorporated; do not overmix.

4. Pour the batter into the prepared pan and spread into an even layer (it will not look like much batter, but it will rise). Bake until the cake is lightly golden and a toothpick inserted in the center comes out clean, about 30 minutes. Transfer to a rack to cool slightly.

5. Carefully remove the cake using the parchment paper and set on a rack. Tear away the paper and let cool completely. (These can be baked a day in advance and kept in an airtight container at room temperature.)

6. To serve, cut the cake into finger-friendly squares (about 2 inches) and generously frost the tops. Set on parchment squares, small doilies, or a platter to serve. Sprinkle with coconut, if desired.

a

b

c

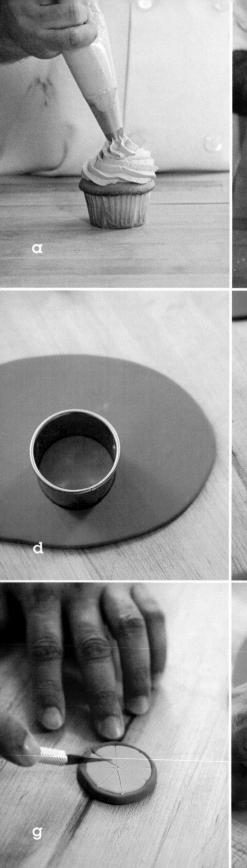

d

e

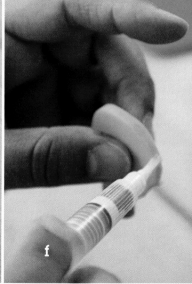

f

g

h

i

COCKTAIL CUPCAKES

{ MAKES 24 CUPCAKES }

These little cocktail-themed cakes are the ultimate dessert for a cocktail party! Each has the color and flavor of a popular cocktail—margaritas, strawberry daiquiris, and piña coladas—with the appropriate fruit garnish made out of fondant. Make these with whatever cupcake you like, but I think vanilla (page 292) is best, to allow the flavors and colors of the toppings to really shine.

There are three basic steps to each variation:
1. Pipe the appropriate buttercream over each of the 24 cupcakes in a swirl pattern (a).
2. Put 2 cups rock sugar in a bowl and roll the frosted edge of the cupcake gently in the sugar (b).
3. Top the cupcakes with the appropriate garnish (c).

FOR MARGARITAS:

Decorator's Buttercream (page 302), with water omitted, recipe adjusted as follows: add ¼ cup plus 2 tablespoons tequila of your choice, plus green food coloring gel at the end to tint the buttercream, in a pastry bag fitted with #6 star tip

1 pound green fondant

1 pound lime-green fondant (6 ounces each of green and yellow fondant kneaded together)

Powdered sugar or corn starch, for dusting a work surface

Water pen

X-ACTO knife or other thin-bladed knife such as a paring knife

1½ inch and 2 inch punches

To make the fondant limes:

1. Dust your work surface with powdered sugar and roll out a small piece of green fondant to ⅛-inch thick. Punch out a 2-inch ring (d), then punch out the center with a 1½-inch ring to create the peel (e).

2. Roll out a small piece of lime green fondant and punch out a 1½-inch circle. Apply water to the edge of the lime green circle with a water pen or pastry brush (f) and put the lime green circle into the dark green ring (g). Press the X-ACTO knife lightly into the lime-green center to make 8 sections.

3. Repeat to make 24 cupcakes, reusing the punched out portion of each ring in the next batch you roll.

4. Use the X-ACTO knife to make an incision that runs halfway up the limes, allowing you to twist them (h). Let them dry before setting them atop the cupcakes (i).

FOR STRAWBERRY DAIQUIRIS:

Decorator's Buttercream (page 302), with water omitted, recipe adjusted as follows: add ¼ cup plus 2 tablespoons rum, plus red food coloring gel at the end to tint the buttercream, in a pastry bag fitted with #6 star tip
12 ounces red fondant
12 ounces green fondant
Powdered sugar or corn starch, for dusting a work surface
Fondant modeling stick or toothpicks
Small star fondant cutter
Water pen

To make the fondant strawberries:

1. Dust your work surface with powdered sugar and roll a small amount of fondant into a ball roughly the size of a marble. Using one finger against about half of the ball, roll it over your palm to shape it into a cone.

2. Using the stick, poke tiny holes or dots all over the berry to resemble seeds.

3. To make the top, roll out the green fondant to about ⅛-inch thick. Cut it out with a very small flower, star, or snowflake cutter.

4. Using a water pen, brush the back of the green strawberry top.

5. Position the berry over the top, and secure it. Repeat to make 24 strawberries. Let the berries dry completely before setting them atop the cupcakes.

FOR PIÑA COLADAS:

Decorator's Buttercream (page 302), with water omitted, recipe adjusted as follows: add ¼ cup plus 2 tablespoons rum (do not tint the buttercream for piña coladas) in a pastry bag fitted with #6 star tip
12 ounces yellow fondant
12 ounces brown fondant
Powdered sugar or corn starch, for dusting a work surface
Fondant shell modeling tool, or toothpicks
Fondant (pizza) cutter
Fork
Small diamond fondant cutter
Water pen

To make the fondant pineapple wedges:

1. Dust your work surface with powdered sugar and roll a small piece of yellow fondant out to roughly ¼- to ½-inch thick. Using the diamond cutter, cut out a diamond shape and then cut the diamond into 2 triangles with the fondant cutter.

2. Roll out the brown fondant to the same thickness as the yellow. Cut a ¼-inch strip that runs the length of side you just cut with the pizza cutter.

3. Use the water pen to attach the brown fondant to the yellow fondant. Then use a fork to "crimp" the brown piece to give it a slightly rough texture.

4. Use the shell modeling tool to scratch some lines in the yellow fondant, creating a pineapple-like texture. Repeat to make 24 pineapple wedges. Let the wedges dry before applying them to the cupcakes.

THANKSGIVING DINNER

Along with the 4th of July, Thanksgiving is one of the two great American holidays. For my family, it's a celebration of everything we have. I love Thanksgiving for many reasons. As the child of immigrants who found the American dream here, I was raised to appreciate the United States and everything it offers those of us who are lucky enough to live here. As a baker and passionate home cook, I also love that this holiday is built around a meal. My family eats together all the time, but Thanksgiving is a meal like no other, bringing with it memories of Thanksgivings past, each dish conjuring up its own associations. In these pages are the Valastros' recipes for all the must-have Thanksgiving dishes, from the turkey and cranberry sauce to an Italian-American stuffing recipe that's been in our family for generations.

HERBED TURKEY WITH HOMEMADE GRAVY

{ SERVES 10 TO 12 }

Turkey with gravy is the centerpiece of most families' Thanksgiving dinner, and it's no different for the Valastros. For us, that turkey is one of the few things other than a cake that we all gather around periodically. (Maybe it's because, like a cake, you carve a turkey before serving it.) For the best results, unwrap the fresh or fully thawed turkey a day in advance, pat it dry with paper towels, and let it sit uncovered in the refrigerator to dry out the skin.

One fresh or thawed frozen 15-pound turkey, giblets and neck removed and reserved
1 bunch fresh rosemary
1 bunch fresh thyme
7 tablespoons unsalted butter, 6 at room temperature
Kosher salt
Freshly ground black pepper
1 head garlic
1 lemon, halved
2 onions, quartered
1 bay leaf
10 whole black peppercorns
1 carrot, peeled and quartered crosswise
1 stalk celery, quartered crosswise
1 tablespoon all-purpose flour

1. Let the turkey rest at room temperature for 2 to 3 hours before roasting.

2. Position a rack in the lower part of the oven and preheat the oven to 400°F.

3. Finely chop 1 tablespoon each of the rosemary and thyme. Put the chopped herbs in a small bowl, add the 6 tablespoons softened butter, season with a pinch of salt and pepper, and stir with a rubber spatula. Set aside.

4. Season the turkey's skin generously with salt and pepper and rub to help it adhere. Lift the turkey skin and smear the herbed butter all over the turkey between the skin and the meat. Stuff the garlic, lemon halves, quarters of 1 onion, and the remaining sprigs of rosemary and thyme into the turkey cavity. Tie the legs together at the base, using kitchen twine.

5. Roast the turkey, rotating the pan once halfway through, for 1 hour. (If the skin darkens too quickly, tent it loosely with foil.) Lower

the oven to 350°F, baste the outside of the turkey all over with some of the juices from the pan and continue to roast, basting every half hour with the pan juices, until a thermometer inserted into the inner thigh registers 155°F, about 1 hour 30 minutes. Remove from the pan and tent the bird with foil; let rest 30 minutes before carving.

6. While the turkey is roasting, start the gravy: Put the turkey giblets and neck in a medium, heavy saucepan. Add the bay leaf, black peppercorns, the remaining onion, and the carrot and celery to the pan, and fill with water just to cover. Bring to a boil over medium-high heat, then reduce the heat to a simmer and continue to simmer until the liquid is reduced by half, about 30 minutes. Strain the stock, and discard the solids.

7. When the turkey is out of the oven, pour the juices from the roasting pan into a fat separator or glass measuring cup; let sit 2 or 3 minutes for the fat to separate. Meanwhile, in a small bowl, rub together the remaining tablespoon of the butter and flour until fully combined. Discard the fat from the pan juices and add the juices to a medium saucepan; set over medium heat. When hot but not yet boiling, add the flour-butter mixture and whisk constantly until incorporated. Pour in the homemade stock, whisking, and bring the mixture to a boil; reduce to a simmer and cook until the gravy is thickened to the consistency you like. Serve hot with the turkey.

Tip: *You can punch up your gravy by stirring in minced fresh herbs such as thyme, rosemary, and/or sage just before serving. Sliced button or wild mushrooms that have been sautéed in butter, along with minced shallots are also a nice addition to the gravy and complement the turkey.*

ROASTED GARLIC MASHED POTATOES

{ SERVES 8 }

These became a family favorite almost by accident one Thanksgiving when my wife, Lisa, was roasting garlic for another recipe, and decided to mash some leftover cloves into the mashed potatoes. If you've never roasted garlic, then you're in for a treat: the raw, oniony flavor of the garlic mellows and sweetens, and the cloves turn mashably soft and a beautiful, burnished brown that looks very cool against the white of the potatoes and the brown of the gravy.

1 large head garlic
1 tablespoon olive oil
1 pound russet potatoes
Kosher salt
¾ cup half-and-half
2 tablespoons unsalted butter

1. Position a rack in the center of the oven and preheat to 425°F.

2. Cut off the top of the head of garlic, exposing the cloves. Set the garlic head in the center of a large (12-inch or so) piece of aluminum foil; drizzle with the olive oil, then fold up the sides of the foil packet and lightly pinch closed; the seal does not have to be especially tight. Set in a small baking dish and roast until the garlic is fragrant and the cloves are tender to a knife tip, 40 to 45 minutes. Remove and unwrap; let rest until cool enough to handle.

3. Meanwhile, peel the potatoes and cut them into 1-inch pieces; immediately place in a large pot and add water to just cover them; season very generously with salt. Bring to a boil over medium-high heat and continue to cook until the potatoes are tender to a knife tip, about 35 minutes. When the potatoes are almost done, gently warm the half-and-half and butter in a small saucepan on the stovetop until the butter is almost melted.

4. Drain the potatoes in a colander, then return to the pot. Squeeze the garlic out of the cloves and add to the pot. Mash well until almost smooth, taking care to not overmash. Add the warmed butter mixture in a thin stream, whisking, until the potatoes are creamy. Season to taste with salt and serve warm.

Garlic Greatness: *Roasted garlic can be a terrific way to add flavor to a number of recipes; spread it on sandwiches along with mayonnaise, or blend it into creamy sauces and vinaigrettes for another layer of flavor.*

SAUTÉED KALE WITH
RED-WINE VINEGAR & ALMONDS

{ SERVES 6 TO 8 }

Shown here with Homemade Cranberry Sauce, recipe on page 214.

Every year, some vegetable or another seems to become the hot item at trendy restaurants around the United States. Recently, kale got to be very popular, which made my family feel like trendsetters, because Italian-Americans have been eating it for generations. If you've never eaten kale, it's pleasantly toothsome, with a lightly peppery flavor that gets along great with strong flavors like the garlic and red-wine vinegar in this recipe. The almonds add crunch, but you can leave them out and this will still be delicious.

In addition to your Thanksgiving turkey, you can serve kale with roasted chicken, beef, or pork.

¼ cup olive oil

5 cloves garlic

3 large bunches curly kale, stems removed and discarded, leaves washed and roughly torn or chopped

Kosher salt

Freshly ground black pepper

¼ cup red-wine vinegar

⅓ cup slivered almonds or pignoli nuts, toasted if desired

1. Heat the oil in a large, heavy pot set over medium-high heat. Add the garlic, and cook over medium heat, stirring occasionally, until the garlic is softened and very lightly browned, 2 to 3 minutes.

2. Add the kale and toss to coat with the oil; season generously with salt and pepper. Pour in the vinegar, toss well with tongs, and turn up the heat to medium-high. Cover and let cook, lifting the lid to toss occasionally, until the kale is wilted, 6 to 8 minutes. Add more salt and pepper if needed.

2. Transfer the kale to a serving plate or platter, and top with the almonds, if desired. Serve warm.

HOMEMADE CRANBERRY SAUCE

[SERVES 8]
Photograph on page 212.

Truth be told, there's nothing wrong with store-bought cranberry sauce, but my sister Mary is positively obsessed with cranberries; so, when it's her turn to host the Thanksgiving celebration, she always makes a homemade version. Her trick is adding some minced ginger to the sauce, which is about as far from Italian-American as you can get, but gives it a subtle but unmistakable zing.

¼ cup plus 1 tablespoon granulated sugar

One 10-ounce bag defrosted frozen cranberries

2 tablespoons orange juice, preferably not from concentrate

One 1-inch piece peeled fresh ginger, minced

Kosher salt

Freshly ground black pepper

1. Put ¾ cup water and the sugar in a medium, heavy saucepan. Set over medium-high heat, and cook, stirring occasionally, until the sugar dissolves, about 3 minutes. Add the cranberries, orange juice, ginger, and a pinch each of salt and pepper. Cook, stirring occasionally, until the cranberries burst and the sauce thickens, about 12 minutes.

2. Remove the pan from the heat and let cool slightly; transfer the cranberry sauce to a bowl and chill until completely cooled. Serve chilled or at room temperature.

VALASTRO FAMILY STUFFING

{ SERVES 16 TO 20 PEOPLE, WITH LEFTOVERS }

This is a truly one-of-a-kind family original, a uniquely Italian-American stuffing made with sausage, bread, mortadella, two types of cheese, tomatoes, eggs, onions, and herbs. The recipe originated with my late Grandmother Madeline and today is made by my sister Mary, who's tweaked it over the years: It eats like a cross between stuffing, a frittata, and a sausage pizza. Be warned: People will flip out when they taste this. It also makes incredible leftovers.

¼ cup olive oil

1 medium yellow onion, coarsely chopped

3 pounds sweet Italian sausage (with or without fennel), casings removed

1 bag (14 ounces) store-bought seasoned stuffing

2 heaping tablespoons finely chopped flat-leaf parsley leaves (from about ½ bunch of parsley)

5 large garlic cloves, chopped

½ pound very finely grated Pecorino Romano (about 2 cups)

1 pound thinly sliced mortadella (preferably without pistachios), cut into 1-inch squares

2 pounds scamorza (dried mozzarella, available from Italian grocers and specialty shops), cut into medium dice (about 4 cups diced)

2 pounds fresh mozzarella, cut into medium dice (about 4 cups diced)

1½ pints cherry tomatoes, halved, seeds squeezed out and discarded, finely chopped

1 cup seasoned breadcrumbs

6 slices white bread, crusts removed and discarded

½ teaspoon freshly ground white pepper

12 large eggs, at room temperature

1 tablespoon baking powder

1. Position a rack in the center of the oven and preheat the oven to 350°F.

2. Heat 1 tablespoon oil in a large heavy skillet over medium-high heat. Add the onion and cook, stirring, until softened but not browned, about 3 minutes. Add the sausage to the skillet and brown it, stirring periodically to ensure even cooking and continue to cook until no pink sausage remains in the pan, about 15 minutes.

3. Meanwhile, fill a large bowl halfway with cold water. Add the stuffing mix, and soak for about 3 minutes. Put the parsley, garlic, Pecorino Romano, mortadella, scamorza, fresh mozzarella, tomatoes, and breadcrumbs in a large mixing bowl. Remove the stuffing from the water in batches, squeeze as tightly as possible to extract as much liquid as possible, and add to the bowl. Run your fingers through the mixture to break up any large pieces.

4. Once the sausage has browned, drain it in a colander and add it to the bowl.

5. Soak the bread under running water, then squeeze it, tear it into pieces, and add it to the bowl. Season the mixture with white pepper.

6. Crack the eggs over the mixture and stir with a wooden spoon or knead, until well incorporated. Add the remaining 3 tablespoons of olive oil and the baking powder and knead or stir again. The mixture should be very moist.

7. Grease a large (at least 12 inches by 17 inches by 2½ inches deep) lasagna pan or other large pan with nonstick cooking spray. (A 16 ⅝-inch x 11 ⅞-inch x 2½-inch deep disposable aluminum lasagna pan is perfect for this; you can also use two smaller pans but try to use similar-sized ones so that the stuffing cooks at the same rate in each one.) Transfer the stuffing to the pan and use a wooden spoon or rubber spatula to spread it out evenly. It will sit low in the pan, but needs room to rise when baked.

8. Bake until the stuffing has risen slightly and is golden brown on top, about 1 hour. Remove it from the oven, let rest for 10 minutes, then serve.

Tip: *To make this stuffing a little richer, dot it with unsalted butter before baking it.*

MOLASSES COOKIES

{ MAKES ABOUT 2½ DOZEN COOKIES }

Spices may not be seasonal, but the spices in these cookies—cinnamon, cloves, and allspice—always put me in mind of fall because they are important ingredients in so many recipes of that season, including the pumpkin pie on page 221. Usually, the scent of sugar rules the air at the Carlo's Bake Shop factory, but in the fall, the factory smells of those spices, which always gets me excited for the holidays.

2⅓ cups all-purpose flour
1½ teaspoons baking soda
Pinch kosher salt
¾ teaspoon ground cinnamon
¼ teaspoon ground cloves
½ teaspoon ground allspice
¾ cup unsalted butter, at room temperature
½ cup dark brown sugar
½ cup granulated sugar, plus more for rolling
1 large egg
1½ teaspoons pure vanilla extract
½ cup molasses

1. Sift the flour, baking soda, salt, cinnamon, cloves, and allspice into a large bowl.

2. Put the butter, dark brown sugar, and granulated sugar in the bowl of a stand mixer and cream them together on medium-high speed until light and fluffy, about 3 minutes. Add the egg and the vanilla and beat to incorporate. Add the molasses and beat until combined.

3. Working in three batches, gradually add the dry ingredients to the wet, mixing on low speed to incorporate between additions. Turn the dough out onto a sheet of plastic wrap; tightly wrap, and chill for 30 minutes and up to overnight.

4. When ready to bake the cookies, position a rack in the center of the oven and preheat the oven to 325°F. Line 2 cookie sheets with parchment paper.

5. Scoop out 2-inch balls of dough and roll them in granulated sugar to coat; place on the baking sheets at least 2 to 3 inches apart. Press each down gently with your fingers to flatten slightly. Bake for 10 to 12 minutes, rotating the cookie sheets halfway through baking.

6. Transfer the cookies to racks to cool; serve right away or keep in an airtight container at room temperature for up to 3 days.

PIECRUST

[MAKES ONE 9-INCH PIECRUST]

This is my recipe for a basic piecrust. While there's nothing wrong with buying a store-bought crust, there's also nothing like making your own; even if it doesn't come out perfectly, your guests will know that your time and attention went into it, and that makes it automatically more special, especially for a holiday like Thanksgiving.

2 cups all-purpose flour, plus more for
   flouring work surface
¾ cup vegetable shortening
1 tablespoon granulated sugar
1 teaspoon fine sea salt
7 tablespoons ice-cold water

1. Put the flour, shortening, sugar, and salt in the bowl of a stand mixer fitted with the paddle attachment. Paddle at lowest speed just until the mixture holds together, about 30 seconds. (You can use a hand mixer if you allow the shortening to soften at room temperature before beginning.) Add 6 tablespoons water, and paddle until absorbed, about 30 seconds. If the dough seems dry or fails to come to-gether, add the last tablespoon of water.

2. Transfer the dough to a piece of plastic wrap and refrigerate for 30 to 60 minutes.

3. Lightly flour a work surface, and roll out the dough in a circle, about 14 inches in diameter (see note) and about ¼-inch thick. Roll it up onto the rolling pin (see note), and transfer to a 9-inch pie pan, unspooling it over the top. Tap the pan gently on the counter and the dough will fall into place. Put your hands at

the 2 o'clock and 10 o'clock positions on the side of the pan, and rotate the pan from just under the lip to cause the excess dough to fall away. (If molded to an aluminum pie pan, the dough can be wrapped in plastic and frozen for up to 2 months. Let thaw to room temperature before filling and baking.)

Blind Baking: *If you need to bake the crust with no filling, fill the pie with dry beans or rice, or set another pie pan in the well, invert, and bake on the center rack of an oven preheated to 350°F until the crust is firm and golden, about 25 minutes.*

How to Roll Pastry onto a Rolling Pin
Put the rolling pin at the far side of the dough and use your fingers to coil it around the pin, then simply roll it up onto the pin.

How to Measure for a Pie Tin without a Ruler
If you don't have a ruler in the kitchen, invert your pie pan over the dough, centering it, making sure you have a 2-inch border of dough around the pan. (You can eyeball 2 inches much more accurately than the 14 inches mentioned in the recipe.)

PUMPKIN PIE WITH AUTUMN LEAVES

{ MAKES ONE 9-INCH PIE, SERVING 10 TO 12 }

I think of pumpkin pie as a perfect storm of autumn flavors because it's made with aromatic spices and a vegetable that screams, "Fall!" During Thanksgiving week, we sell countless pumpkin pies to customers who have been serving our dessert at their holiday tables year after year. This is our recipe, with one extra touch: Leaves are punched out of pie dough and arranged around the crust of the pie to underline the time of year.

You will need a leaf plunger cutter to make the leaf-shaped cookies.

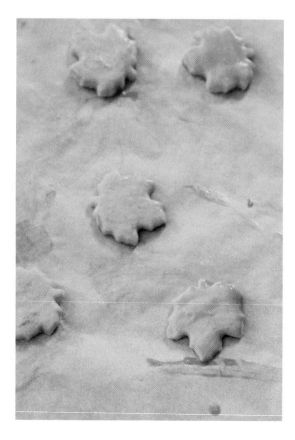

1 can (15 ounces) pumpkin puree
    (I like Libby's Pure Pumpkin)
¾ cup granulated sugar
1½ teaspoons cornstarch
½ teaspoon fine sea salt
1 teaspoon ground cinnamon
¼ teaspoon ground cloves
¼ teaspoon ground ginger
¼ teaspoon ground nutmeg
¼ teaspoon ground allspice
¼ teaspoon ground mace
1 teaspoon pure vanilla extract
1½ cups whole milk
2 extra-large eggs, at room temperature
1 unbaked 9-inch pie crust (recipe follows),
    trimmed dough saved for leaves, or 2
    store bought 9-inch pie crusts
2 cups Italian Whipped Cream (page 311),
    or store-bought whipped cream (optional)

a

b

1. Position a rack in the center of the oven and preheat the oven to 450°F.

2. Put the pumpkin, sugar, cornstarch, salt, cinnamon, cloves, ginger, nutmeg, allspice, mace, and vanilla in the bowl of a stand mixer fitted with the paddle attachment. Paddle at low-medium speed for approximately 2 minutes.

3. With the motor running, pour in the milk in 2 additions. Stop the motor, scrape the sides of the bowl with a wooden spatula, restart, and paddle for an additional 2 minutes. Add the eggs and paddle until absorbed, approximately 2 additional minutes.

4. Pour the mixture into a 9-inch piecrust in a pan, and bake for 15 minutes, then lower the heat to 375°F, and bake until a finger dabbed onto the surface emerges clean, 30 to 40 minutes.

5. Remove the pie from the oven and let cool for 1 to 2 hours.

6. Meanwhile, punch leaves out of the leftover piecrust dough, if using homemade, or from the extra store-bought piecrust, if using store bought. Arrange the leaves on a lightly greased baking tray and bake until lightly golden brown, 8 to 10 minutes.

7. Once the leaves are cool, arrange them around the perimeter of the pie, affixing them in place with dabs of buttercream (a). If desired, pipe or spoon whipped cream in the center of the pie (b) and serve more whipped cream alongside.

CHRISTMAS EVE

Christmas Eve has to be one of the best nights of the year to be a parent. There's just nothing like the anticipation that young children have for the arrival of Santa Claus and the opening of presents on Christmas morning. When I think of Christmas Eve, I remember my own sleepless nights waiting for Saint Nick, as well as tearing open the wrapping on my gifts Christmas morning. As far as food goes, I have to be honest: For the longest time, we didn't really have a memorable Christmas Eve dinner in my parents' home, or even in my own home until the last few years, because we're a baking family and we always had to run the business, both on Christmas Eve and on Christmas Day. It wasn't until a few years ago that we began to close up shop on December 25, and enjoy a real family dinner on the 24th. And so, I can't say that the following recipes are traditions in my family, but they are the dishes that I used to crave on Christmas Eve when my family had to work and which I'm happy to say we're able to enjoy together as a family today.

LINGUINI WITH WHITE CLAM SAUCE

{ SERVES 6 }

Shown here with Zucchini Fritters, recipe on page 228.

On Christmas Eve, my family sometimes serves a traditional Italian Feast of the Seven Fishes, made up of (at least) seven fish and shellfish dishes. The classic linguini with clam sauce was often part of the menu, an especially Hoboken-appropriate touch since clam dishes have a rich history in my hometown. (Frank Sinatra, a Hoboken native, loved clams Posillipo.)

This recipe can be served year-round: at the holidays kick off a meal with a small plate of it, maybe with a glass of Champagne or Prosecco; in the summer, serve it with a glass of well-chilled white wine.

8 cloves garlic, thinly sliced
2 tablespoons extra-virgin olive oil
Three 8-ounce bottles clam juice
3 dozen fresh littleneck clams, cleaned
Kosher salt
1½ pounds linguini
½ cup chopped fresh flat-leaf parsley
3 tablespoons freshly squeezed lemon juice

1. Bring a large pot of salted water to a boil.

2. Meanwhile, sauté the garlic in the olive oil over medium-low heat until softened, 2 to 3 minutes. Add the bottled clam juice and season lightly with salt.

3. When the pasta water is boiling, salt it, and add the linguini. Cook until *al dente* (see note).

4. Meanwhile, bring the clam sauce to a boil and add the rinsed clams. Cover the pot and let cook, stirring occasionally, until the clams are thoroughly opened, about 10 minutes. (Discard any clams that have not opened.)

5. Drain the pasta and return it to the empty pot. Add the clam sauce, lemon, and half the parsley to the pot (reserve the clams); toss with tongs to coat and moisten.

6. Transfer the pasta and juices to a large serving bowl or 6 wide, shallow bowls. (The pasta dish should be brothy, with lots of sauce.)

7. Place the opened clams atop the pasta, and sprinkle the dish with the remaining parsley.

Note: *If the clams are large, chop half or all of the clam meat and mix into the pasta; discard any empty shells.*

Al Dente: Al dente *means "to the tooth," and it's how we Italians like to eat our pasta. To achieve al dente pasta, a good rule of thumb is to shave a minute or two from the cooking time on the box.*

ZUCCHINI FRITTERS

{ MAKES ABOUT 16 }
Photograph on page 226.

If you love potato pancakes, try the Italian-American answer to that starter and make these zucchini fritters, which capture the flavor of this underappreciated vegetable in a savory patty. Serve these as a starter on their own, or as a side dish with fish and meats.

2 large zucchini, grated on the large holes of a box grater (about 3½ cups)
1 teaspoon kosher salt
1 tablespoon all-purpose flour
2 tablespoons unseasoned breadcrumbs
1 large egg, lightly beaten
1 tablespoon finely chopped fresh flat-leaf parsley
Finely grated zest of ½ lemon (about 1 teaspoon)
Freshly ground black pepper
Canola or olive oil, for frying

1. Put the grated zucchini in a fine-mesh strainer. Sprinkle with ¾ teaspoon kosher salt and let sit in the sink or set over a bowl to draw out some of the excess moisture, 30 minutes to an hour. Squeeze the zucchini as dry as possible using paper towels or a clean hand towel.

2. Transfer the zucchini to a large bowl, discarding the juices, and sprinkle with the flour and breadcrumbs. Add the egg and toss to combine. Add the parsley, lemon zest, and a pinch or two of black pepper, and toss until incorporated.

3. Heat a large nonstick skillet over medium heat and add 1 tablespoon of oil. When the oil is hot but not smoking, working in two batches, add small scoops of the zucchini batter (1½ to 2 tablespoons each) to the pan at least 1 to 2 inches apart; flatten each gently with the back of an offset spatula. Let cook, turning halfway through, until the outsides are well browned and crispy and the insides are cooked through, 6 to 7 minutes total. Remove and drain on paper-towel–lined plates. Serve warm.

GARLIC BREAD

{ SERVES 8 }

This is one of the straight-up, all-time, gotta-have-it Italian-American staples: served to start meals, to dunk in pasta sauces, and as an accompaniment to main courses. This is how we make it in my family, with the bread wrapped in foil to trap that garlicky goodness inside, then unwrapped at the end of the baking to crisp it up. It'll fill your home with that wonderful garlic smell, whetting the appetite of one and all.

4 large cloves garlic, minced
½ stick unsalted butter
Pinch kosher salt
1 baguette, sliced open
Chopped fresh flat-leaf parsley, for garnish

1. Position a rack in the center of the oven and preheat the oven to 350°F.

2. Put the garlic and butter in a small, heavy saucepan and add a pinch of salt. Cook, stirring, until the butter is fully melted and bubbling and the garlic is fragrant. Remove the pan from the heat.

3. Using a pastry brush, spread the cut baguette with the butter until saturated. Place the cut sides back together and wrap the loaf in foil. Cook on a baking sheet until warmed, about 5 minutes. Open the foil, place the baguettes cut-side up in the pan, and bake until the top is toasted, about 5 more minutes.

4. Remove the bread from the oven and and garnish with the parsley. Slice thickly and serve hot.

GARLIC & ROSEMARY PRIME RIB

{ SERVES 10 TO 12 }

Few dishes scream special occasion like a prime rib roast: a cut of meat that's meant to serve a large group. In this recipe, a garlic and rosemary paste is inserted into little slits in the beef; when the meat is roasted that flavor melts into it, filling it with herbaceous flavor.

One 4-bone prime rib roast (about 9 pounds), from the loin end if possible, fat trimmed

5 cloves garlic

Kosher salt

3 tablespoons finely chopped fresh rosemary

6 anchovies packed in oil, finely chopped, optional

Olive oil

1 tablespoon very coarsely ground black pepper

¼ shallot, minced

1. Remove the roast from any wrappings or butcher paper and season lightly with salt. Let rest at room temperature for 2 hours before cooking.

2. Position a rack in the center of the oven and preheat to 425°F. On a cutting board, mince the garlic and sprinkle with a pinch of salt. Using the edge of a sharp chef's knife, smash the garlic into a paste. Add the chopped rosemary and anchovies, if using, and a drizzle of olive oil.

3. Transfer the roast to a roasting pan with the fatty side up and the bones facing down. Season generously with salt. Make a few 1-inch slits in the roast using a sharp knife and stuff them with some of the garlic mixture; a good trick is to set the blade of the knife in the slit and slide the filling in, pressing it in with a finger. Rub the remaining mixture, and a little more olive oil, all over the beef. Rub the pepper all over the beef.

4. Cook, rotating the pan once, until the roast is browned on top, about 25 minutes. Lower the heat to 350°F and continue to cook, rotating the pan every half hour or so, until a thermometer inserted into the thickest part reads 130°F, 1 hour to 90 minutes. Remove and transfer the meat to a cutting board, tent loosely with foil, and let rest 15 to 20 minutes.

5. Meanwhile, add a tablespoon of oil to a small saucepan, heat it over medium-high heat, add the shallot, and cook, stirring, for 1 minute. Pour the juices from the roasting pan into a fat separator or glass measuring cup; wait for the fat to rise to the top, about 1 minute. Discard the fat and pour the juices into the saucepan. Add more beef broth if you need more sauce.

6. Carefully cut the roast off the bones, then very thinly slice from the short end. Serve with the sauce.

RICOTTA CHEESECAKE

{ SERVES 8 TO 10 }

Generally speaking, there are two kinds of cheesecake: Italian ricotta cheesecake and creamy New York cheesecake. This recipe is a crowd-pleasing combination that blends the best of both worlds—the ricotta cheese from the Italian version and the cream cheese and graham cracker crust from the New York style—for a melting-pot dessert that will feel familiar and homey to just about everybody.

FOR THE CRUST:

1 stick (½ cup) unsalted butter, melted

2 cups graham cracker crumbs (from about 14 crackers)

2 tablespoons granulated sugar

⅛ teaspoon kosher salt

FOR THE CHEESECAKE:

3 cups full-fat ricotta cheese

1 cup cream cheese

⅔ cup granulated sugar

6 large eggs

1 cup heavy cream

2 teaspoons pure vanilla extract

Zest of 1 small orange

Pinch ground cinnamon

2 tablespoons all-purpose flour

1. Position a rack in the center of the oven and preheat the oven to 400°F.

2. Make the crust: Put the butter, graham cracker crumbs, sugar, and salt in the bowl of a food processor and pulse until finely ground. Remove and, using your fingers, press the mixture onto the bottom and sides of a 10-inch pie dish. Bake until lightly browned, about 10 minutes. Remove the crust from the oven and let cool.

3. Meanwhile, in the bowl of a stand mixer, beat the ricotta and cream cheese with the sugar. Add the eggs, heavy cream, and vanilla and beat until smooth. Add the orange zest, cinnamon, and flour and beat just to incorporate.

4. Lower the oven temperature to 350°F. Pour the mixture into the cooled crust and transfer to the oven. Bake until just set but not browned, about 45 minutes. Remove and let cool completely; refrigerate until ready to serve, then slice.

CHOCOLATE FONDUE

{ SERVES 4 TO 6 }

Chocolate fondue is something my family only used to eat at restaurants, but we loved it so much that we invested in a fondue set and began making it at home. Fondue is something that most people think of as a great way to eat cheese (and it is), but we Valastros love using it as a changeup come dessert time: You make the fondue, and dip chocolate-friendly foods such as fruit, pretzels, and cubes of pound cake into it. Kids love it, and it brings out the kid in any adult, which is the perfect way to end a Christmas Eve dinner.

FOR THE FONDUE:

½ cup heavy cream

2 tablespoons unsalted butter

1 tablespoon cognac or brandy (optional)

½ teaspoon pure vanilla extract

One 4-ounce bar bittersweet chocolate, chopped

One 4-ounce bar semisweet chocolate, chopped

Pinch kosher salt

FOR DIPPING:

Chopped cantaloupe

Fresh strawberries

Bite-sized Rice Krispies Treats

Cookies

Pretzel rods

Pound cake, cut into bite-sized pieces

1. Put the cream, butter, cognac (if using), and vanilla extract in a medium saucepan over medium-low heat and cook until simmering.

2. Turn off the heat and add the chocolate and a pinch of salt; stir with a wooden spoon or heatproof spatula until the chocolate is fully melted and the mixture is smooth. (Place back on the heat briefly as needed.) Transfer to a fondue pot to keep warm. Serve with your favorite dippers and fondue forks for dipping.

CROQUEMBOUCHE

{ SERVES 12 }

This is my Italian-American take on a French dessert that's usually made with choux pasty puffs held together by caramel. The Valastro version is a way more decadent affair, with cream puffs filled with espresso-tinged pastry cream, then topped with cream, espresso powder, and chocolate shavings. These are small but rich so I like to serve one croquembouche to every two guests and let them share it; I always say that there's nothing like dessert to bring families together, and this takes that idea to the next level.

11 cups Lobster Tail Cream (double the
   recipe on page 310), made without
   the Bailey's Irish Cream, in a pastry bag
   fitted with #7 star tip
4 tablespoons espresso powder or
   finely ground espresso (such as that found
   in premeasured pods for espresso
   machines), plus more to taste
24 Cream Puff Shells (page 241)
2 cups store-bought chocolate shavings

a

b

d

e

1. Put the lobster tail cream in a large mixing bowl. Put 2 tablespoons of the espresso in a small heatproof bowl and add 2 tablespoons of hot water. Stir them together into a paste, then whisk the paste into the lobster tail cream. Taste, and if desired, make more paste with equal parts espresso powder and hot water and whisk into the cream for a stronger espresso flavor.

2. Fill the puffs: Use your pinkie to hollow out the puffs from the bottom. Put a few cups of cream into a pastry bag fitted with #7 star tip, and pipe cream into the puffs from the bottom, refilling the bag with cream as you run out (a, b).

3. Pipe some of the cream into the center of each of 6 small dessert plates. Arrange 3 cream puffs around the cream (c) and 1 cream puff on top. Working with 1 plate at a time on a turntable, pipe more cream over and around the cream puffs (d). Turning the turntable, use a cake spatula to smooth the cream and completely encase the cream puffs (e). Sprinkle a teaspoon of espresso powder over each dessert (f) and finish by garnishing with chocolate shavings.

CREAM PUFF SHELLS

{ MAKES ENOUGH FOR 24 CREAM PUFFS }

These are the light, airy shells produced from choux pastry dough, that are the foundation of Carlo's Bake Shop's famous cream puffs. For traditional cream puffs, fill them with Italian Custard Cream (page 306), following the instructions on page 283. Three cups of cream will fill 24 puffs.

6 tablespoons unsalted butter
⅛ teaspoon fine sea salt
1 cup all-purpose flour
4 extra-large eggs

1. Put 1 cup water, the butter, and salt in a heavy saucepan and bring to a boil over high heat. Add the flour and stir with a wooden spoon until the ingredients come together into a smooth, uniform dough, approximately 2 minutes.

2. Transfer the mixture to the bowl of a stand mixer fitted with the paddle attachment. (If you don't have a stand mixer you can use a hand mixer fitted with the blending attachments.) Start paddling on low speed, then add the eggs, 1 at a time, until thoroughly absorbed, mixing for 1 minute between each egg, and stopping the motor periodically to scrape down the sides and bottom of the bowl with a rubber spatula. Finish with the final egg and mix for an additional 2 minutes. (Use the dough immediately. It does not refrigerate well.)

3. Position a rack in the center of the oven and preheat the oven to 450°F.

4. Transfer the dough into a pastry bag fitted with #6 plain tip. Pipe rounds on 2 nonstick baking trays, about 2 inches in diameter by about ½ inch high, leaving 2 inches between each puff. You should be able to make 24 puffs.

5. Bake the puffs in the oven, in batches if necessary, until golden brown, 15 to 20 minutes.

6. Remove the tray from the oven and let the puffs cool in the tray for 20 minutes. The puffs can be kept in an airtight container at room temperature for up to 2 days before filling and serving.

CHRISTMAS DAY

Christmas Day is 100 percent pure happiness, from kids opening presents to piling into the car and making the rounds, driving on empty highways and backstreets to visit family in other houses around New Jersey. This isn't a day when you want to do a lot of cooking, because, after all the shopping and wrapping of presents, you want to just decompress and enjoy your family. I recommend a buffet menu, setting out food that visitors can snack on as they drop by. This menu includes some of my favorites, such as a marinated seafood salad and baked ziti, both of which are perfect for grazing, or for bringing along to a pot luck at another house, and the cake at the end is the ultimate Christmas indulgence, lavishly decorated to look like a holiday present.

MARINATED SEAFOOD SALAD

{ SERVES 6 }

Seafood salads are something I've been eating since I was a little kid. They're one of the all-time most popular Italian-American dishes, eaten at home, in restaurants, and at salad bars. What I love about them is that they are easy to cook—you just poach the different seafoods, chill them, and dress them with a simple vinaigrette—but give you a wide variety of textures and flavors. When it comes to entertaining, this salad is an asset because the seafood can be cooked up to two days ahead of time, then dressed and served at the last minute.

2 pounds large or jumbo shrimp (peeled and deveined), thawed if frozen

2 pounds cleaned squid, tentacles trimmed off and reserved, bodies sliced into ½-inch rounds

1½ pounds fresh mussels, beards cleaned and shells scrubbed

1 cup drained canned scungilli, coarsely chopped

¾ cup finely chopped celery, preferably tender inner stalks

¼ cup freshly squeezed lemon juice, plus the finely grated zest of ½ lemon

¼ cup extra-virgin olive oil

Kosher salt

Freshly ground black pepper

2 tablespoons capers packed in brine

2 tablespoons fresh oregano leaves, coarsely chopped

1. Bring a medium-large pot of water to a boil over high heat. Fill 2 large bowls halfway with ice water and have them near the stove. Add the shrimp to the boiling water and cook until firm and pink, about 2 minutes. Remove with a small strainer or slotted spoon and transfer to an ice water bowl. Bring the pot of water back to a boil and add the squid. Cook until opaque, about 1 minute 30 seconds, then transfer to the ice water with the shrimp. Bring the water back to a boil and add the mussels; cook until the shells are opened widely, 4 to 6 minutes. Discard any that do not open; remove the others to the fresh ice bowl. (Alternatively, you can rinse all the seafood in a large colander under cold running water until cooled.)

2. Remove the mussels from the shells. Drain all of the seafood well and add it to a large serving bowl with the chopped scungilli. (The seafood can be prepared and combined a day or two in advance; refrigerate in an airtight container and dress just before serving. If seafood is chilled, let come to room temperature for 10 to 15 minutes before dressing and serving.)

3. Scatter the celery, lemon juice, and zest, the olive oil, a generous pinch each of salt and pepper, the capers, and the oregano over the seafood and toss well.

4. Serve family style or divide among small plates.

BAKED ZITI

{ SERVES 6 TO 8 }

Whenever the whole family gets together, there's always a pasta, and baked ziti is one of my favorite classics. This is a simple recipe, but all of the essential elements—garlic, tomato, basil, and two types of cheese (mozzarella and pecorino Romano)—are in perfect balance.

2 tablespoons olive oil

5 cloves garlic, thinly sliced

Two 28-ounce cans crushed tomatoes,
    or plum tomatoes, crushed by hand,
    with their juice

1 cup loosely packed fresh basil leaves,
    plus more for garnish

Kosher salt

Freshly ground black pepper

Crushed red-pepper flakes to taste, optional

1½ pounds dried ziti

⅔ cup grated pecorino Romano cheese

2 pounds shredded mozzarella

1. Heat the olive oil in a medium pan over medium-high heat. Add the garlic and cook, stirring, until lightly browned, about 3 minutes. Carefully pour in the tomatoes and juices. Puree with a handheld blender, or in batches in a stand blender.

2. Return the sauce to the pot and stir in the basil and a generous pinch each of salt and pepper, and the crushed pepper, if using. Bring to a simmer over medium heat, and cook, stirring occasionally until hot and slightly darkened in color, 25 minutes. Turn off the heat and let cool slightly.

3. Meanwhile, position a rack in the center of the oven and preheat to 375°F. Bring a large pot of salted water to a boil, add the ziti, and cook until almost *al dente* (usually about 2 minutes less than the cooking time on the package directions); drain and return to the empty pot.

4. Spread a thin layer of the sauce over the bottom of a deep, 9-inch by 13-inch glass baking dish. Toss the rest with the pasta and half of the pecorino Romano. Pour the pasta mixture into the baking dish and flatten out slightly with the back of a spatula. Sprinkle evenly with the mozzarella and the remaining pecorino Romano.

5. Bake until the cheese is melted and lightly golden, and the sauce is hot and bubbling, about 35 minutes. Remove and garnish with more basil. Let cool slightly and slice into squares, or serve piping hot in bowls with a serving spoon.

CHERRY-GLAZED HOLIDAY HAM

{ SERVES 8 TO 10 }

Like the rib roast on page 231, a glazed ham is one of those creations that was made for holiday entertaining.

One 7 to 8 pound smoked, cured, bone-in ham
⅓ cup cherry preserves
2 tablespoons dark brown sugar
1 tablespoon freshly squeezed lemon juice
½ teaspoon freshly ground black pepper
¼ teaspoon dried thyme
¼ teaspoon kosher salt

1. Position a rack in the lower half of the oven to make room for the ham and preheat to 325°F. Starting at one side and working horizontally across the top and upper sides, shallowly score the ham with a sharp knife in 1-inch sections. Repeat vertically down the top and upper sides of the ham.

2. Transfer the ham to a nonstick or foil-lined roasting pan. Cook about 20 minutes per pound, until a thermometer inserted into the thickest part of the ham (not touching the bone) registers 130°F, about 2 hours 20 minutes total.

3. Meanwhile, in a small saucepan, whisk together the cherry preserves, brown sugar, lemon juice, black pepper, thyme, and salt. Bring to a simmer over medium-high heat and cook until slightly thickened, 1 to 2 minutes.

4. When the ham is cooked, remove it from the oven and, using a pastry brush, carefully coat the ham on the top and sides with the cherry mixture. Return to the oven and turn up the heat to 425°F. Cook until the glaze is sizzling and slightly browned, about 8 minutes. Remove and let the ham rest 15 to 30 minutes before slicing and serving.

CANDY CANE COOKIES

{ MAKES ABOUT 24 COOKIES }
Shown here with Gingerbread Cookie Sandwiches, recipe on page 252.

Visually speaking, these are very cool cookies, which resemble candy canes by twisting red and white strands together like a barber-shop pole. When the holidays roll around every year, Lisa and the kids whip up a huge batch of these, then invite all the cousins over for a last-second party.

These taste even better the day after you bake them, and will keep for about a week and a half in an airtight container.

2 cups all-purpose flour
½ teaspoon baking powder
⅛ teaspoon kosher salt
⅓ cup unsalted butter
⅓ cup vegetable shortening
1 large egg
¾ cup granulated sugar
1½ teaspoons pure vanilla extract
About 16 drops red food coloring

1. In a medium bowl, combine the flour, baking powder and salt; set aside.

2. In the bowl of a stand mixer, beat the butter and shortening together at medium-high speed. Add the egg, sugar, and vanilla extract and beat to incorporate on medium speed. Add the flour mixture and mix on low speed until just incorporated.

3. Divide the dough evenly into two balls. Wrap one in plastic wrap. Place the other in a medium bowl and add the red food coloring a few drops at a time, mixing and squishing the dough with your hands to help the coloring incorporate. (Warning: You will have pink fingers!) When all the food coloring is worked in, wrap the dough in plastic wrap; refrigerate both doughs until slightly firm, about 1 hour.

4. Position a rack in the center of the oven, preheat the oven to 375°F, and line 2 large baking sheets with parchment paper.

5. Grab a small chunk of one of the doughs (about 1 tablespoon) and roll it on a clean work surface into a thin tube (about ¼- to ½-inch-thick). Trim to about 4 inches in length. Repeat with the other color of dough. When you have two tubes in two different colors, lay them side by side on the work surface and roll them together gently to stick. Twist them to form a spiral of color, then shape one end into a hook shape to form a candy cane. Transfer to the prepared baking sheets. Repeat with the remaining dough.

6. Bake until the cookies are just set but not yet browned, 8 to 10 minutes. Remove and let cool on the baking sheet for 3 to 5 minutes; then transfer carefully to racks to cool completely.

GINGERBREAD COOKIE SANDWICHES

{ MAKES ABOUT 16 SANDWICHES }
Photograph on page 250.

All the kids in our family used to get together and make these cookies
at our house every year; now we do it at the Carlo's factory.

FOR THE COOKIES:

3½ cups all-purpose flour

1½ teaspoons baking soda

¼ teaspoon kosher salt

1½ teaspoons ground ginger

1 teaspoon ground cinnamon

¼ teaspoon ground cloves

¼ teaspoon ground allspice

1 cup unsalted butter, at room temperature

1 cup (firmly packed) dark brown sugar

½ cup granulated sugar

1 large egg

¼ cup molasses

FOR THE FILLING:

⅓ cup unsalted butter, at room temperature

½ teaspoon pure vanilla extract

⅛ teaspoon kosher salt

1½ cups confectioners' sugar

1 tablespoon milk, plus more as needed

1. In a large bowl, combine the flour, baking soda, salt, and spices; set aside. In the bowl of a stand mixer, beat the butter and sugars together until they appear light and fluffy. Add the egg and mix to combine. Add the molasses and mix to combine, scraping down the sides of the bowl once if needed.

2. Working in three batches, add the dry ingredients, mixing between each addition until just incorporated. Remove the dough and turn it out onto a sheet of plastic wrap; form into a disk, wrap tightly and refrigerate until firm, at least 2 hours. (Dough can be made up to 1 day ahead.)

3. Preheat the oven to 350°F. Remove the dough and cut it in half. Re-wrap one half and place back in the fridge; let the other sit at room temperature a few minutes to soften slightly. Lightly flour a work surface and your rolling pin, and roll out the dough to ¼-inch thick.

4. Line a baking sheet with parchment paper.
    Using cookie cutters, cut out the gingerbread
    men, and transfer to the prepared sheets.
    (If the dough feels very soft, refrigerate the
    gingerbread men on the baking sheet for
    15 minutes before placing in the oven to
    bake.) Bake until cookies appear firm and like
    they're just starting to crisp, 12 to 15 minutes.
    Remove and let cool on the sheet 5 minutes,
    then transfer to racks to cool completely.

5. Meanwhile, make the sandwich filling. Beat
    together the butter, vanilla, and salt until
    fluffy. Add the confectioners' sugar in 2
    batches and beat on low speed until incorpo-
    rated. Add the milk and beat until the mixture
    is thick but spreadable, adding more milk in
    1 teaspoon increments as needed. Spread
    some of the icing onto half of the cooled
    gingerbread men; sandwich each with another
    cookie.

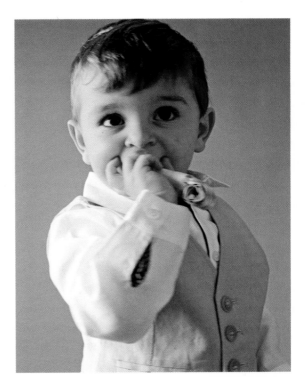

EGGNOG ICE CREAM

{ MAKES ABOUT 6 CUPS }

Two of my favorite treats in one bowl! I just love eggnog. It's one of those things that's only available in the supermarkets for a few weeks each year, which makes it feel special, and making it into an ice cream really puts it over the top. You can serve this on its own, make a sundae with it, or blend it into a milkshake.

1¼ cups milk

7 large egg yolks

¾ cup plus 2 tablespoons granulated sugar

1¾ cups heavy cream

2 tablespoons dark rum

¼ teaspoon ground nutmeg

¼ ground cinnamon, plus more for serving

⅛ teaspoon ground cloves

1. Put the milk in a medium, heavy saucepan and bring to a boil over medium heat. Meanwhile, in a bowl, beat the egg yolks and sugar together.

2. When the milk comes to a boil, remove the pan from the heat. Ladle a small amount (about 3 or 4 tablespoons) into the egg mixture, whisking constantly, to temper the yolks. Once incorporated, stream in the rest of the warm milk, whisking constantly.

3. Transfer the mixture to the saucepan and place over low heat; cook, whisking constantly, until the mixture is slightly thickened (it should coat the back of a spoon), about 5 minutes. Remove and strain through a fine strainer into a heatproof bowl. Stir in the heavy cream, rum and spices. Cover and refrigerate until chilled, about 2½ hours.

4. Remove the mixture and transfer to an ice cream maker; prepare according to the manufacturer's directions. Transfer to a storage container and sprinkle with cinnamon. Freeze until firm, 1 to 2 hours.

CHRISTMAS GIFT CAKE

{ MAKES ONE 10-INCH-SQUARE CAKE }

This is a holiday cake to end all holiday cakes, shaped and decorated like a gift box, with a big, shiny red bow on top. We first created a version of this cake for Mother's Day several years ago, but it's just as at home during the holidays.

Three 10-inch-square cakes of your choosing (pages 292 to 298), filled with your choice of filling (pages 302 to 311)

6 cups white Decorator's Buttercream (page 302) in a pastry bag fit with #8 plain (interchangeable) tip (Do not use the tip to dirty-ice the cake; page 287.)

36 ounces white fondant

1 canister (4 ounces) gold luster dust

2 to 3 ounces grain alcohol (such as Everclear) or vodka

About 1 pound green fondant

2 pounds red fondant. About 1½ cups red Decorator's Buttercream in a pastry bag fitted with a #6 plain tip

TOOLS & EQUIPMENT

14-inch by 14-inch wooden platform

10-inch cardboard square

Textured rolling pin

X-ACTO knife, or sharp, thin-bladed knife such as a paring knife

Fondant ribbon cutter

3-inch pegs or 3-inch-high can (see instructions)

Steamer

Water pen

1. Set a 14-inch by 14-inch wooden square, about ¼-inch thick, on your turntable. Top with a 10-inch cardboard square and prepare a triple-layer 10-inch-square cake (3 layers of cake, 2 of frosting, for a 4½-inch high cake) on the square, filling it with the filling of your choice and dirty-icing it (page 287).

2. Roll out the white fondant to ⅛-inch thick. Roll over it with a textured rolling pin to create a wrapping-paper look (a). Drape the cake with the fondant, smooth it in place (b), and trim it (pages 287 to 289).

3. Create gold paint by putting the gold luster dust in a small bowl and stirring in just enough grain alcohol to turn it into a paint. Paint the cake until it is uniformly gold and let it dry briefly (c).

4. Pipe some white buttercream onto the wood around the cake and spread it out with a cake icing spatula. Cut four strips of green fondant, each 14 inches by 4 inches, and lay them on the platform around the cake (d). (After laying down the first piece, trim each successive piece prior to laying them down to keep from overlapping them; you want them to be flush with each other.) Steam the seams where the pieces meet and gently press together with your fingers to smooth out the seam.

a

b

c

d

e

f

g

h

i

5. Roll out about half the red fondant to at least 18 inches long and 1¾ inches wide. Use the strip cutter to cut four 18-inch long strips, each 1½ inches wide. Pipe a line of buttercream up and over the cake in its upper third, crossing it with another line running down the cake. Set the streamers on the buttercream to create a "ribbon." Trim the streamers (e).

6. Roll all remaining red fondant out to a ¼-inch-thick rectangle about 6 inches by 9 inches. With the ribbon cutter still set to 1½ inches, cut: one 9-inch strip, one 3-inch strip, and two 6-inch strips.

7. Turn the 9-inch strip over and use the water pen to apply a thin layer of water to the center inch.

8. Lift the outer ends of the strip (f) and bring them to the center, setting them down end to end and forming loops. Press down gently to make sure they adhere to the damp center portion of the strip (g).

9. Turn over the 3-inch strip and use the water pen to dampen the entire upward-facing surface. Set it between the loops, perpendicular to the looped 9-inch strip (h).

10. Put your thumb and index fingers in the loops and flip the ribbon over. Fold the 3-inch center strip over and dab with water to seal it neatly around the center of the bow.

11. Flip the two 6-inch strips over and cut 1-inch triangles at one end of each strip to make them look like the ends of ribbons.

12. Position the 6-inch strips like ribbons extending from the center of the cake, where the streamers cross, and positioning the triangle ends furthest from where the bow will rest. Use the water pen to cause the ribbons to ripple, fixing them to the cake in two or three places for support (i).

13. Position the bow in the center of the cake, where the ribbons and streamers meet, fixing it in place with a dab of water.

14. Steam the cake all over with the steamer to give the box top and box a nice, shiny, uniform look.

15. Using the red buttercream, rotate the turntable and pipe a shell border around the bottom of the cake.

NEW YEAR'S EVE BUFFET WINNERS

Years mark the time in our lives, and when it's time to turn the page and move on from one year to the next, a big celebration is in order! The menu here is of my favorite party foods, plain and simple. There are figs in blankets (wrapped in puff pastry), that combine savory and sweet in each bite, little pizzettes (miniature pizzas) that are perfect for passing, a champagne cocktail that is Lisa's preferred drink on December 31, and a taste of the old country in the sausage and lentil combination that is eaten on New Year's Eve in Italy for luck. The pink elephant cake has a funny backstory: They say that when you drink too much you see pink elephants, but you can keep that one to yourself, because the elephants are fun and festive on their own, without the story. You can also leave them out and the cake will still be exciting and delicious.

CHAMPAGNE & STRAWBERRY COCKTAILS

{ SERVES 8 }
Photograph on page 270.

If there's one night of the year when you simply have to have Champagne, it's New Year's Eve. A bubbly, cold glass of the stuff is all you ever really need, but for a special night like this, I think you have to go the extra mile and dress it up. (Maybe it's the cake decorator in me.) Here, the rims of the Champagne glasses are dusted with sugar and mashed strawberries and lemon juice are added to the bottom of the glasses for extra flavor and color. This is a guaranteed crowd-pleaser and one of Lisa's favorite drinks. Cheers!

2 cups fresh ripe strawberries, stemmed and finely chopped, chilled
Juice of 1 large lemon
¼ cup granulated sugar
1 bottle Champagne or sparkling white wine

1. Put the chopped strawberries in a bowl and lightly smash the fruit using a fork; set aside.

2. Pour the lemon juice into a small shallow bowl. Add the sugar to a small shallow dish or bowl. One by one, turn 8 to 10 champagne glasses upside down and dip in the lemon juice, then transfer to the sugar; twist in the sugar to coat the rim.

3. Spoon 1 to 2 teaspoons of the chopped strawberries and about ¼ teaspoon lemon juice into the bottom of each glass. Top with champagne or sparkling wine and serve.

LENTILS WITH ONIONS

{ SERVES 8 }

Lentils are a New Year's Eve tradition in Italy, where they are served alongside a pork sausage, cotechino (page 268). I'm really excited to share them with you, because I've always felt like lentils are underrated in the United States. Like white beans, they take on the flavor of whatever they're cooked with, but they're a more surprising choice because most people here are only used to seeing them in a soup, if at all. They are delicious with roasted pork and game dishes, and even with white-fleshed fish, and leftovers—if there are any—can be eaten at room temperature.

1 tablespoon unsalted butter
1 yellow onion, peeled and thinly sliced
Kosher salt
4 cloves garlic, peeled and thinly sliced
2⅔ cups dried lentils
⅔ cup red wine
2 bay leaves
2 to 3 sprigs fresh thyme
3 to 4 sprigs fresh flat-leaf parsley
Freshly ground black pepper

1. Melt the butter in a medium, heavy sauté pan over medium-high heat. Add the onion and season with salt. Cook, stirring, until softened and lightly browned, 8 to 10 minutes, adding the garlic after 5 minutes.

2. Stir in the lentils, then add the red wine and cook, stirring once or twice, until the liquid has mostly evaporated and been absorbed by the lentils, about 2 minutes. Add the bay leaves, thyme, and parsley; season with salt and a generous amount of pepper. Add just enough water to cover (about 4 cups), and bring to a simmer. Cover the pot and adjust the heat to maintain a simmer; cook, adding more water as needed (mixture should be moist, but not soupy), until the lentils are tender, about 40 minutes. Remove the herb sprigs and bay leaves before serving.

SLICED ZUCCHINI & TOMATO PIZZETTE

{ MAKES 16 SLICES }

I've never been intimidated by making pizza at home, but, then again, I'm a baker! The more fans I meet around the country, the more I learn how many people don't feel like they can succeed in making pizza at home. If that describes you, try making these little pizzettes: They're made with frozen puff pastry, don't need to be cooked on a pizza stone, and are light, so they leave room for dinner (and Champagne) on New Year's Eve, or any occasion you serve them. Everybody in my family—kids and adults alike—love these little starters, and I'm sure your family will, too.

One 14-ounce sheet frozen puff pastry, thawed

8 ounces part-skim or full-fat mozzarella (scant 2 cups)

2 medium zucchini, washed and thinly sliced

1 cup grape or small cherry tomatoes (about 16), halved lengthwise

½ red onion, quartered, then very thinly sliced

1. Position a rack in the center of the oven and preheat to 475°F.

2. Cut the pastry sheet into 16 equal rectangles. Stretch the dough slightly so they form squares, then press down lightly with your fingertips to make a pizza-crust-like border. Arrange the squares on a nonstick baking pan or two.

3. Fill the pressed-down centers with cheese (about 2 scant tablespoons shredded mozzarella each). Then top with 2 or 3 thin slices zucchini, 2 or 3 tomato halves, and a sprinkling of red onion.

4. Bake until puffed, crisp and browned at the edges, 10 to 12 minutes. Remove, transfer to a platter and serve warm.

FIGS IN BLANKETS

{ MAKES ABOUT 18 }

Shown here with Cotechino Sausage, recipe on page 268.

One of my personal favorite snacks: You've heard of pigs, or hot dogs, in blankets, but what about figs in blankets? These puff-pastry–wrapped fruit bites are subtly sweet; the figs bake well, softening and almost melding with the pastry. These fall somewhere between a savory and a sweet, so it makes perfect sense that they are drizzled with honey and sprinkled with salt.

1 large egg, beaten
1 sheet frozen puff pastry, thawed
1 pint container fresh figs, halved lengthwise,
    tough ends trimmed
Honey, for drizzling
Kosher salt

1. Position a rack in the center of the oven and preheat the oven to 425°F. Line a baking sheet with aluminum foil.

2. Add 1 tablespoon of cold water to the egg, stir together, and set aside.

3. Use a pizza cutter to cut out as many 3-inch-long, 2-inch-wide strips from the puff pastry as fig halves you have. Pick up a fig and hold it cut-side-up in one hand; with the other hand, wrap a piece of puff pastry around the fig, stretching the dough so it covers most of the bottom of the fig. Brush the inside of one pastry end with some of the egg wash and press tightly to seal. (The fig should look like it's sitting cut-side up in a little puff pastry nest.) Repeat with the remaining figs and puff pastry strips.

4. Drizzle the cut side of the fig lightly with some of the honey, and sprinkle with salt. Bake until the puff pastry is golden and the fig looks moist and melty, about 20 minutes. (Check the pan after 15 minutes; if the figs are very juicy and their juices seem to be scorching on the bottom of the pan, shift the figs slightly with a spatula into a fresh spot.)

5. Remove the baking sheet from the oven, let the figs rest for 2 minutes, then arrange on a plate or platter and serve.

COTECHINO SAUSAGE

{ SERVES 8 }
Photograph on page 266.

My first memory of these pork sausages are from New Year's Eve when I was a kid. They were one of my first lessons about life in my family's ancestral home, because my grandmother Grace told us that they were served on New Year's Eve back in Italy, along with lentils (page 263), and they were supposed to bring you good luck in the coming year. Fortunately, these sausages are also delicious, especially cooked as they are here, plumped in chicken broth, then sautéed in a garlicky oil. After you try these you may discover what my family has known for generations: You won't want to wait a year before making these again!

2 fresh (uncooked) cotechino sausages,
    about 1 pound each
1 quart chicken broth
1 bay leaf
2 tablespoons vegetable oil
2 cloves garlic
Lentils with Onions, optional

1. Unwrap the cotechino and pierce the casing in a few places with the tines of a fork or the tip of a knife. Transfer to a large saucepan and add the chicken broth and the bay leaf; add water as needed to cover the sausage. Bring the liquid to a boil over high heat, then lower the heat to maintain a simmer and cook the sausage until cooked through, about 1 hour. Drain and let rest until cool enough to handle. (This can be done 1 day ahead; wrap the sausage in plastic wrap and refrigerate.)

2. Transfer to a cutting board and slice into ½-inch-thick rounds. Heat a large nonstick skillet over medium-high heat and add the oil; add the garlic and cook until lightly browned, about 3 minutes. Remove the garlic and, working in batches if needed, slide the sausage rounds into the hot pan (they should sizzle when they touch down). Cook, turning once, until lightly seared and golden on both sides, 4 to 6 minutes total cooking time.

3. Serve the sausage slices from a platter. If serving the lentils alongside, serve them from a bowl in the center of the platter.

TIPSY TIRAMISÙ CUPS

{ MAKES 8 }

Shown here with Champagne & Strawberry Cocktails, recipe on page 262.

Tiramisù means "pick me up," and the Italian dessert that goes by that name, made with ladyfingers soaked in espresso or coffee, are a favorite in my family, and something we sometimes call on for a jolt of sugar, coffee, and carbs during a long day at the bakery. In this version, a little brandy is added to make these festive and appropriate for New Year's Eve; you can make a nonalcoholic version by simply leaving it out. Rather than topping these with a traditional coating of cocoa powder, I use just a few chocolate shavings, which looks nicer and doesn't distract from the rest of the dessert.

2 cups heavy cream
¼ cup confectioners' sugar
Two 8-ounce containers mascarpone
1 cup espresso or very strong brewed coffee, fully cooled
1 tablespoon brandy or dark rum
24 ladyfingers
Semisweet chocolate bar, for shaving

1. In a stand mixer or using a hand mixer, beat the heavy cream and confectioners' sugar until soft peaks form. Add the mascarpone and whip just to incorporate, about 30 seconds. Scrape down the bowl and remove from the mixer.

2. Put the espresso and the brandy in a small bowl and stir them together. In the bottom of each of 8 martini glasses or other small glasses or stemless white wine glasses, break up 2 ladyfingers to form a thick layer. Using a spoon, drizzle each layer with some of the espresso mixture (the cookies should be fully soaked). Top each with an equal layer of the cream mixture, spreading it evenly into the glass with the back of the spoon. Repeat the layering once, soaking the second layer of ladyfingers with the remaining espresso mixture.

3. Top the glasses with a sprinkling of chocolate shavings. Refrigerate at least 15 minutes or up to 4 days before serving. (If storing overnight or longer, cover with plastic wrap before chilling.)

POACHED PEARS WITH VANILLA GELATO

{ SERVES 8 }

Poached pears are an elegant dessert for any special occasion meal in the fall, and they're ideal for entertaining because the pears can be poached up to 2 days in advance, and make their own syrupy sauce when cooked. Most important, the pears are delicious: sweet but not too sweet, with a natural shape that fits beautifully into glass dessert cups or onto a shallow dessert plate These can be set out at a buffet, or served at the most formal of dinner tables.

1 lemon, halved
1½ cups granulated sugar
4 firm-ripe pears, preferably Bosc
2 cinnamon sticks
1 bay leaf
1 vanilla bean, split lengthwise
Vanilla gelato, for serving (about 2 pints)
Fresh raspberries, for serving

1. Pour 5 cups of water into a large, high-sided skillet or saucepan. Add a squeeze of lemon juice. Add the sugar and set over medium-high heat, stirring occasionally, until the sugar is dissolved and the liquid appears syrupy.

2. Meanwhile, carefully peel the pears, then halve them lengthwise and core them. Add them to the syrup along with the cinnamon sticks, bay leaf, and vanilla bean. Maintain a simmer and let cook until the pears are tender when pierced with a sharp, thin-bladed knife, 15 to 30 minutes, depending on the ripeness of the pears. (They will continue to soften slightly as they cool.) Turn off the heat and let the pears cool in the syrup.

3. Serve the pears warm or store in an airtight container fully submerged in the syrup for up to 2 days. Place a generous scoop of vanilla gelato next to the pears, and top with a few fresh raspberries. (If any of the pears won't stay on their backs, cut a small flat spot into the most bulbous part to help steady them.)

HOMEMADE NUT & FRUIT BRITTLE

{ SERVES 10 TO 12 }

People don't make brittle at home very often. It seems difficult, like something that is supposed to be pumped out by a factory machine, not produced by human hands. But brittle is actually very easy to make, and, as with most things, nothing tastes as special as when you make it yourself. This brittle combines fruit and nuts for something more unexpected than peanut brittle with additional layers of flavor.

You can package this in cellophane bags, tied at the top with ribbon, as take-away treats for your guests, or serve it at a buffet or in candy bowls around your New Year's Eve party.

¼ cup (2 ounces) salted butter,
   plus more for greasing
2 cups granulated sugar
¼ cup light corn syrup
2 cups fruit-and-nut trail mix (or a homemade
   blend of peanuts, almonds, dried
   cranberries, and pepita seeds)

1. Line a baking sheet with parchment or wax paper, then lightly grease with butter.

2. Put the sugar and ¼ cup water in a medium, heavy-bottomed saucepan and stir them. Add the butter and corn syrup and clip a candy or deep-fat thermometer securely to the side of the pan. Cook over medium-high heat, stirring once or twice with a heatproof spatula, until the mixture is boiling. Raise the heat slightly and continue to boil until the candy becomes deep brown and registers 350°F on the thermometer, about 22 minutes. (In the last minute or so of cooking, watch it closely; the temperature will begin to rise very quickly, and, if it rises above 360°F, the brittle will start to taste a bit burnt.)

Remove the pot from the heat, then carefully fold in the trail mix with a wooden spoon or heatproof spatula, not letting the hot caramel splash. Be careful, it is hot.

3. Immediately pour the mixture out onto the prepared pan, starting in the center and quickly spreading and smoothing as you go with the spoon or the heatproof spatula. (For the prettiest results, don't mess with the candy too much once it starts to set.) Let cool completely, at least 2 hours. Break the candy into shards or cut it into triangles using a sharp knife. Store in an airtight container.

MIDNIGHT COOKIES

{ MAKES ABOUT 2 DOZEN }

This is a variation on black and white cookies designed just for New Year's Eve. They make terrific party favors (wrapped in cellophane) or the perfect dessert for a kids' dinner earlier in the evening, before the adult festivities begin.

FOR THE COOKIES:

4 cups cake flour
½ teaspoon baking powder
¼ teaspoon kosher salt
1 cup unsalted butter, softened, plus more
    for greasing
1¾ cups granulated sugar
4 large egg whites
¼ teaspoon pure vanilla extract
½ teaspoon lemon extract
¾ cup whole milk

FOR THE ICING:

4 cups confectioners' sugar
¼ cup plus 2 tablespoons milk
3 tablespoons unsweetened cocoa powder
One large tube white decorating frosting

1. Position a rack in the center of the oven and preheat the oven to 375°F.

2. Sift the flour, baking powder, and salt together into a medium bowl.

3. Put the butter and sugar in the bowl of a stand mixer and beat them on medium-high speed until light and fluffy. Add the egg whites and beat to combine. Add the extracts and beat to combine. Alternate adding the dry ingredients and the milk in 3 additions, mixing between additions until just combined.

4. Lightly grease 2 cookie sheets with butter. Stagger 3-tablespoon scoops of the batter onto the sheets, leaving about 3 to 4 inches between. Wet a small offset spatula or butter knife with water, and use it to spread each ball of batter into a thin round, creating as smooth a surface as possible. Continue to wet the spatula as needed.

5. Bake the cookies until fluffy and lightly golden, 8 to 10 minutes, rotating the baking sheets in the oven halfway through. Remove and let cool on wire racks.

6. Meanwhile, make the icing. In a small bowl, stir together the confectioners' sugar, milk, and vanilla until smooth. Stir in the cocoa powder. Using a small offset spatula or butter knife, spread the icing over the cookies. Using the white decorating frosting, pipe the design of a clock onto each cookie (the numbers 12, 3, 6, and 9, and two arrows pointing to indicate that it's almost midnight). Let set in a cool place for at least 30 minutes before serving. The cookies may be served right away or refrigerated in an airtight container for up to 2 days.

NEW YEAR'S EVE CAKE

{ MAKES ONE 9-INCH CAKE }

New Year's Eve demands something special for dessert; after all, it's the last one you'll eat all year, or the first one of the New Year if you don't serve it until after midnight. This cake has two ideas going on at once: On top of the cake is a clock striking midnight. On the side of the cake is a scattering of fondant confetti, and a parade of pink elephants wearing party hats and blowing into noisemakers. (The truth is that I got the idea for this cake from the old expression that if you drink a lot, you begin to see pink elephants, which seems appropriate for New Year's Eve.) For a simpler cake, just leave off the elephants and go with the clock theme and confetti.

One 9-inch cake of your choosing (pages 292 to 298), frosted and filled with the filling of your choice (pages 302 to 311)
24 ounces black fondant
About 1 pound white fondant
White Decorator's Buttercream (page 302), in a pastry bag fitted with #6 or #7 plain tip
About 1 pound pink fondant
4 ounces blue fondant
4 ounces green fondant
4 ounces purple fondant

TOOLS & EQUIPMENT

Steamer
Letter impression set
X-ACTO knife, or other sharp, thin-bladed knife such as a paring knife
Elephant cutter or mold
Water pen
3 edible markers, any bright, cheerful colors

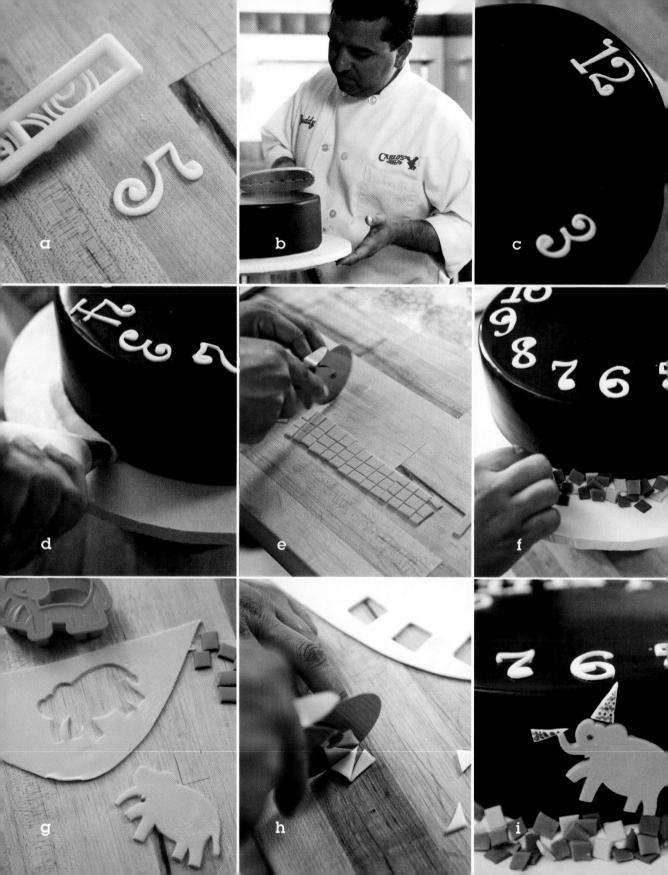

a

b

c

d

e

f

g

h

i

1. On a turntable, prepare a double-layer cake on a doily-lined cardboard circle, filling it with the filling of your choice and dirty-icing it (page 287).

2. Drape the cake with black fondant, smooth it in place with the smoother, and trim it (page 289).

3. Roll the white fondant out, ¼-inch thick. Use the number stencil from the letter impression set to cut out numbers 1 through 12 (a). Steam the cake (b) and put the numbers on the cake, placing the 12, 3, 6, and 9 first to ensure even spacing (c). Steam the cake again to make the numbers shiny. Pipe the hands of the clock, about to strike midnight, with the buttercream, or cut them out of fondant and apply them with a water pen. (If using fondant, do not steam the cake for the second time until after applying the hands.)

4. Pipe a border around the bottom of the cake with white buttercream (d). Roll out 3 ounces of the pink fondant, the blue, green, and purple fondant to ⅛-inch-thick rectangles and cut small (¼-inch) squares using an X-ACTO knife, or use a 1-inch-square punch to punch squares out of the fondant, then use a pizza cutter to cut each square into smaller squares (e). Arrange the squares generously around the bottom of the cake, adhering them to the buttercream, so that they resemble confetti (f).

5. Roll out the remainder of the pink fondant ⅛-inch thick and punch out 6 elephants with a mold (g). Affix the elephants to the side of the cake using a water pen.

6. Make the party hats and noisemakers (h):

   • Roll out the remaining white fondant to ⅛-inch thick.

   • Punch out four 1-inch squares with a punch, then cut each square into 3 triangles with the X-ACTO knife, so you have 12 rectangles.

   • Use the edible markers to draw dots on the hats and noisemakers.

7. Use a water pen to apply 2 triangles to each elephant, 1 as a hat and the other as a noisemaker.

8. Use an edible marker to set a dot, representing an eye, on each elephant (i).

APPENDIX

DECORATING

Decorating cakes, cupcakes, cookies, and pies isn't as tough as it looks. It may take a little practice, but if you follow these tips and guidelines, you will be able to successfully create the desserts in this book.

Basic Tools and Equipment for Cake and Cupcake Decorating

Most cakes need to be filled and/or iced, so the most important skill to develop for working with cakes and cupcakes is working with a pastry bag and a turntable. Here's what you need to know.

The Turntable

To pipe neat, even circles on a cake, a turntable is a must. (When I say "cake" here, I'm talking about cakes or cupcakes.) When you use a turntable, the goal is to create a dynamic similar to a machine: Your arm stays in one place, the table turns, and the pressure you place on the bag evenly deposits cream or icing on the cake. Your wrist might turn, or your hand might move up and down to create certain effects (although not for the cakes in this book), but your arm will always be stationary. So, if you don't have one already, get yourself a good, sturdy professional-caliber turntable that will endure for years. (For turntables and other supplies, I recommend Cake Boss products.)

Before starting to work with a cake on a turntable, set it on a doily on top of a round piece of cardboard the same diameter as the cake, and center the cake before going to work on it. (If it's not centered, you will end up with a "wobble" effect.)

As for turning a turntable, you can go clockwise or counterclockwise, although generally speaking, right-handed decorators tend to turn clockwise; lefties, counterclockwise.

Using a Pastry Bag

Fill pastry bags about two-thirds full, being sure to squeeze the contents as far down into the bag as possible, so that they can be forced out of the tip with the slightest pressure.

The proper way to hold a pastry bag is with one hand, resting the weighty, full part of the bag on your forearm and leaning the back of the bag against your upper arm or shoulder for support. This will keep one hand free for turning a turntable or performing other side tasks.

Using a pastry bag well is all about pressure. Generally speaking, when you use the bag, you will apply either steady pressure, for creating long lines or piping filling and/or frosting, or a pulsating pressure for creating borders and shapes.

There are three main pressure techniques called for in this book.

- **Squeeze-and-pull:** This technique involves squeezing and pulling the bag upward to deposit the contents in a dab or blob. The classic example is piping cream puff batter (page 238); in cake decorating, we use this technique to create bulbs and dots that punctuate cakes and cupcakes, such as on the Spiky Layer Cake on page 55.

- **Steady pressure:** This technique, which involves squeezing the bag for a sustained period of a few seconds, is used to produce a continuous line or circle of frosting or cream, such as the bottom border of the New Year's Eve cake on page 279.

- **Pulse:** This technique involves squeezing and pulling with pulse and movement—for example, to create a shell border (see box) around the base of a cake.

A NOTE ON PASTRY BAG TIPS

Generally speaking, you should have a #6 plain and #7 star pastry tip, at the least. For decorating the more show-stopping cakes in this book, you will need special tips. Some recipes call for interchangeable tips, which are small tips shaped to produce special effects such as grass or a basket weave and are affixed to pastry bags with a coupler that acts as a dock or port for them. In addition to the effects they create, these tips are convenient; if you need to create different effects with the same color icing, you don't need to fill different bags, you just change the tip. If a recipe does not indicate "interchangeable" then you just drop the desired tip (a regular pastry tip) into the bag before filling it with the desired icing or frosting.

Shell Border

A shell border can be made with a number of different regular or interchangeable tips, and in just about any size or shape. To pipe a shell border (page 105 for an example), position the tip at the bottom of the cake. Squeeze and pull as you slowly rotate the turntable. Continue all the way around until you return to the starting point.

Preparing Cakes for Decorating

My basic cake recipes are found starting on page 291, and basic frostings and fillings on page 301.

Trimming & Cutting Cakes

Whether you're working with icing or fondant (pages 283 to 289), the first step in decorating any cake is trimming and cutting it. Use a serrated knife to remove the top layer of discolored "skin" of browned cake to make a flat top. If the cake you're making requires you to cut it in half horizontally, first set it on your turntable or work surface. Kneel or bend so that the cake is at eye level and you can get a good head-on look at it. Keep your eye fixed on the point where the knife enters the cake and as you apply pressure to the top with your free hand, rotate the cake against the knife, keeping it straight to get a nice, even cut. If you will be filling the cake, always try to make the layers level with each other, trimming if necessary so they will rest straight when stacked.

Filling and Icing Cakes

I like to use a pastry bag to fill cakes because it reduces the amount of spreading and scraping required to fill and ice a cake neatly and, if you're using a thick cream for a filling, using a spatula to apply the icing might cause the cake to break.

Freezing Cakes

Because it makes the cake easier to cut evenly, and because freezing also makes it firmer, thus easier to halve, ice, and decorate; I like to work with a frozen cake. Freezing a freshly baked and cooled cake also seals in all the moisture, whereas they can dry out in the refrigerator. Cakes should be frozen for 1 to 2 hours for the best trimming texture. You can freeze them for longer, but they will become very hard and should be allowed to thaw slightly before you try to cut into them; check that the cake has a little give to it before you start trimming. Do not try to trim a cake that's hard as a rock because the knife can slip, very dangerously.

Filling Cakes

To fill a cake using a pastry bag, fit the bag with the #6 plain tip. Set the first layer of cake on the turntable. Apply steady pressure (page 283) to pipe the filling in concentric circles, stopping to lift the bag after completing each circle. After the layer is covered with frosting circles, use an icing spatula (see box) to gently smooth it out into an even layer. Carefully set the next layer on top, gently pressing down to ensure it's level. Then lay down the next layer of filling in the same manner.

The balance of flavors and textures varies from cake to cake based on the type of filling you choose. While there's always room for interpretation and personal taste, I find that Chocolate Ganache (page 309), Italian Buttercream (page 305), Vanilla Frosting (page 303), Chocolate Fudge Frosting (page 304), and Cream Cheese Frosting (page 307) are all relatively dense and rich, so the best ratio of filling to cake is 1:2, meaning a layer of filling should be about half the height of a layer of cake. On the other hand, Italian Custard Cream (page 306), Italian Whipped Cream (page 311), Lobster Tail Cream (page 310), and My Dad's Chocolate Mousse (page 308) are relatively airy, so the proper ratio of filling to cake is 1:1, meaning a layer of filling and a layer of cake should be about the same height.

Icing (Frosting) Cakes

Before icing a cake, double-check to be sure the layers look nice and straight and aligned, and be sure the cake is centered on your turntable. If necessary, trim the layers to level them, or use a little extra icing under uneven layers to straighten them.

Put the frosting in a pastry bag fitted with a #6 or #7 star tip. You can use either tip for icing a cake; the #7 will give a slightly larger piping effect. For dirty-icing with Decorator's Buttercream, described on page 287, the #6 tip is the more logical choice.

Spinning the turntable, apply steady pressure to the bag to pipe concentric circles on top of the cake, stopping and lifting the bag between circles. Then, also spinning the table, pipe frosting around the sides, starting at the top and working your way down.

Use the icing spatula to smooth the circles on top of the cake together, by holding the spatula parallel to the cake top, and spinning the turntable, gradually lowering the surface of the spatula close to the cake. Turn your spatula perpendicular to the cake and smooth the sides, again gradually moving the spatula closer to the cake. (For a ridged effect, such as the one on the Fourth of July Flag Cake on page 171, use a decorator's comb; page 286.)

Finally, while spinning the turntable, hold the spatula parallel to the top of the cake and lower it just to smooth the top one last time to level it off and ready it for decorating.

Icing Spatula

For filling and icing cakes, I use an 8-inch icing spatula. Some books recommend an offset (angled) spatula, but I find that the straight shape of an icing spatula gives a greater feeling of control.

Decorator's Comb

A decorator's comb, also sometimes called a *triangle*, can be used to add ridges to the side of a cake. Hold the comb flush against the cake, with the bottom edge against the turntable, and rotate the turntable.

Decorating with Fondant

Several of the cakes, and a few cupcakes and cookies, in this book are covered with fondant and/or decorated with design elements made with fondant. Fondant is a sugar dough that can be purchased in different colors, and it's something we use a ton of at Carlo's, because it creates a smooth and beautiful surface for a cake, and can also be manipulated to make everything from numbers to people to animals to go on top, or around the sides, of the cake. Most people assume that fondant is difficult to work with, but in many ways it's easier to work with than frosting and buttercream: You don't have to mix it yourself, it can be held at room temperature, and you can simply cut shapes from it to make designs.

The colors of fondant called for in the cakes in this book are all available in the Cake Boss line. (In a few cases, you will have to knead two or more colors together to create a color called for in a particular cake.) They are available in 24-ounce and 4-ounce boxes. You should decide how much of each color to buy; this depends on what cakes you plan or are likely to make. If you buy another brand of fondant, use the pictures that accompany the cakes to determine the closest approximation to the desired color.

Fondant Tools

A good basic set of tools for working with fondant includes:

- **Polyurethane or ball-bearing rolling pin:** For rolling out fondant as smoothly as possible.

- **Water pen:** A professional tool that lets you apply dabs of water that act as glue with fondant. (If you don't have one, in most cases—except when working with very small pieces—you can use a pastry brush to apply water.)

- **Fondant (pizza) cutter and/or sharp, thin-bladed knife, such as an X-ACTO or paring knife:** For trimming fondant and cutting shapes.

- **Fondant ribbon cutter set:** The only dependable way to cut strips of various sizes from fondant.

- **Fondant smoother:** This iron-shaped device is used to smooth the top of fondant-draped cakes.

- **Ruler:** For precision.

- **Paint brush:** For applying petal dust and other elements/ingredients to fondant.

- **Steamer:** To finish any fondant design, you can steam the fondant in order to evaporate the cornstarch (or powdered sugar) and give it a smooth, shiny look. You can do this with a fabric steamer, or even an inexpensive travel iron. Pass the steamer 1 or 2 inches over the cake, gently waving it to distribute the steam, until the fondant glistens slightly with moisture. Let the fondant air dry; this should take only a few seconds. Be careful not to let the steamer spit or spray water onto the cake.

STORING FONDANT

Keep fondant in the airtight container it comes in, at room temperature, until you use it. After removing the portion you plan to work with, store the remaining fondant, if any, in an airtight plastic bag in the container at room temperature.

Working with Fondant

- Wash your work surface. Fondant is a magnet for anything and everything—crumbs, debris, or anything else on your work surface will become embedded in the fondant. Even if you manage to get these particles out, they will leave little divots in the surface that cannot be patched over cleanly. So before beginning, brush your surface, wipe it down with a damp cloth, then dry it thoroughly.

- Before working with fondant, knead it for 1 minute to loosen it and activate the gums.

Coating a Cake with Fondant

Dirty-Ice the Cake

Dirty-icing the cake, readies it to receive the fondant. I think of it as similar to a primer coat of paint. Dirty-icing a cake means to frost the cake with a thin layer of Decorator's Buttercream (page 302) to help the fondant stick to the cake. (Most bakers call this a crumb coat because you can see crumbs through the icing.) Dirty-icing doesn't have to be perfect; the main thing is that it covers the entire cake.

To dirty-ice a cake, first ice it as you usually would; see "Icing (Frosting) Cakes," page 285. Then use a piece of poster board to finish the job (see "Icing with Cardboard," page 288), getting as close to the cake as possible.

After dirty-icing a cake, refrigerate it until the buttercream stiffens, 30 to 60 minutes.

SAVING BAGS

Many of the theme cakes in this book call for white (uncolored) decorator's buttercream to be used in both dirty-icing the cake and piping some design elements, usually with an interchangeable tip. To avoid using two different bags—one fitted with the #6 star tip for dirty-icing, the other with an interchangeable tip—pipe the buttercream for dirty-icing with a bag fitted with the coupler, but not tip, then attach the interchangeable tip called for in the decorating instructions. This alternative is noted in the directions for the cakes to which it applies.

Icing with Cardboard

If you don't have an icing spatula on hand, you can do a very clean job using a piece of poster board. In fact, when you dirty-ice a cake prior to working with fondant, finishing the job with a piece of poster board is essential. To do this, cut a 4-inch by 3-inch piece of poster board with very sharp scissors. As you rotate the turntable, hold the edge of the cardboard flush against the edge of the cake. Then turn your attention to the top of the cake, combing in with brushstrokes from the edge of the cake, only halfway across at first, then all the way across. Professional decorators actually prefer this technique because it puts your hands in closer contact with the cake itself, giving you greater control than with a spatula, although less seasoned decorators will probably have greater success icing their cakes in two steps—first using a cake icing spatula, then finishing with the poster board.

Roll Out the Fondant

This is a very important step that requires you to roll out the fondant as thinly, smoothly, and evenly as possible. We use a sheeter at Carlo's, but you can get a similar effect at home with focus and a little practice:

- Dust your work surface with cornstarch or powdered (10X) sugar. Some people use flour, which is a fine alternative, but cornstarch is smoother and lighter, and easier to brush or steam off when you're finished.

- Remove the fondant required from its storage bag/tub. To coat a two-layer, 9-inch cake—which most of the cakes in this book are—begin with a 24-ounce piece.

- Knead the fondant for about 1 minute to activate the gums and make it pliable. If you're working in cold weather, wash your hands in warm water before beginning; warm hands make this job go faster. Just be sure to dry them thoroughly before starting to knead.

- Dust your work surface with more cornstarch; do this as often as necessary when you work to keep the fondant from pulling or sticking.

- Flatten out the ball of fondant with the palm of your hand. Begin rolling it, preferably with a polyurethane rolling pin (second choice would be a sturdy, ball-bearing rolling pin), really putting your forearms and weight into the rolling motion. Lift the fondant up off the work surface frequently to keep it from sticking; cornstarch helps here, but too much cornstarch will cause the fondant to dry out by drawing out its moisture. The heat from your hands helps with this. Get into the habit of rubbing the fondant constantly to keep it from drying out.

- Once you have rolled the fondant out to a length of 18 inches, turn the piece horizontally and fluff it, moving it around to pick up excess cornstarch from the work surface on the bottom. Then roll the other way. As the fondant begins to take on a circular shape, vary the angle of your rolling, first in one direction, then the other. Continue in this fashion until you have rolled a near-perfect circle, ⅛-inch thick, or thinner if you're able. The more you turn the fondant, the thinner and more uniform the result will be.

- Check the fondant for air pockets (bubbles), poking with a needle tool, or a toothpick. After doing this, smooth out the fondant by hand or with a smoother.

Apply the Fondant to the Cake

- Set the rolling pin at the far edge of the fondant circle and roll it back toward you, spooling the fondant up onto the pin and gently knocking off any excess cornstarch. Bring the pin over the cake, unspooling the fondant and lowering it over the other side, letting it drape over the sides and onto your work surface.

- Smooth the top with a smoother, then pull and press down gently on the sides to make the fondant taut all around.

- Caress the fondant with your hands to smooth it against the cake, stretching and pulling it tautly over the top and down the sides, turning the cake and using your fingers to be sure it's smooth all over. Use a pizza cutter or sharp, thin-bladed knife such as a paring knife, to cut around the base and remove any excess fondant. Lift the excess ring up and over the cake. Ball up the excess fondant and return it to its storage bag; it can be reused.

- Put the cake on a turntable. Use a smoother to smooth out the fondant on the top and sides. Inspect the cake; if you find any dry spots (they will appear arid and veined), rub a little vegetable shortening over them, then smooth with the smoother.

You are now ready to decorate your cake.

NOTES ON MAKING FONDANT CAKES

The choice of cake and fillings for the cakes in this book is entirely up to you. Most are best made with vanilla or chocolate cake, but you can try them with other types of cake, such as Red Velvet Cake (page 298) or Carrot Cake (page 296). There is a list of ingredients, tools, and equipment included for each fondant cake recipe. But there are certain items you will need for most recipes, thus they are not listed. These are:

- Cornstarch or confectioners' sugar for dusting your work surface whenever you are rolling out fondant (page 288), or as otherwise indicated

- Turntable

- Cake icing spatula

- Doily-lined cardboard circle

BASIC CAKE RECIPES

The following recipes produce our most popular cakes at Carlo's Bake Shop. Because it's the most common size called for throughout the book, the recipe yields indicate two 9-inch cakes, but these recipes can also be used to produce two heart-shaped cakes, a 13 by 9-inch rectangular cake, or two Bundt cakes using 8-inch-wide, 3-inch-deep molds.

Note that oven temperatures differ, so be sure to follow the signs for doneness (not just cooking time); depending on elevation, weather conditions, and other factors, baking times can vary. Unless otherwise indicated, it's a good idea to have all ingredients at room temperature.

Many of these recipes feature a yield for cupcakes as well. Bake cupcakes at 360°F to prevent them from crowning.

VANILLA CAKE

{ MAKES TWO 9-INCH CAKES OR 24 CUPCAKES }

This vanilla cake recipe, adapted from the one we use at Carlo's, is a good, safe choice for most filled cakes. The custard is optional, but really makes the cake moist and helps prevent it from drying out.

2½ cups cake flour, plus more for flouring the cake pans

2 cups sugar, plus more for unmolding the cakes

2 cups Italian Custard Cream (page 306), optional

¾ cup vegetable oil

2¼ teaspoons baking powder

1 teaspoon pure vanilla extract

½ teaspoon fine sea salt

4 extra-large eggs

1 cup milk

Unsalted butter (about 2 tablespoons) for greasing the cake pans (nonstick spray or vegetable oil may be used)

1. Position a rack in the center of the oven, and preheat to 350°F.

2. Put the flour, sugar, custard cream (if using), vegetable oil, baking powder, vanilla, and salt in the bowl of a stand mixer fitted with the paddle attachment. (If you don't have a stand mixer, you can use a hand mixer, but take extra care not to overmix.) Mix on low speed just until the ingredients are blended together, a few seconds, then raise the speed to low-medium and continue to mix until smooth, approximately 1 additional minute.

3. With the motor running, add one egg at a time, adding the next one after the previous one has been absorbed. Stop the motor periodically and scrape the bowl from the bottom with a rubber spatula to integrate the ingredients, then return the mixer to low-medium speed.

4. After all the eggs are added, continue to mix for 1 additional minute to ensure the eggs have been thoroughly incorporated. This will help guarantee that the sugar is dissolved, and that the flour has been thoroughly mixed in, which will help produce a luxurious mouth-feel in the final cake.

5. With the motor running on low speed, add the milk, ½ cup at a time, stopping the motor to scrape the sides and bottom between the two additions. Continue to mix for another 1 minute or until the mixture appears smooth. Before baking, be sure the batter is between 70° and 73°F, or the cake will crown. (Test by plunging a kitchen thermometer into the center of the batter; if it is too warm, put the bowl in the refrigerator for a few minutes; if too cool, let it rest at room temperature.)

6. Grease two 9-inch cake pans (2 inches deep) and flour them. (For more, see "How to Flour a Cake Pan," below.)

7. Divide the batter evenly between the two cake pans, using a rubber spatula to scrape down the bowl and get as much batter as possible out.

8. Bake until the cake begins to pull from the sides of the pan and is springy to the touch, 25 to 30 minutes.

9. Remove the cakes from the oven and let cool for at least 30 minutes, preferably 1 hour. The cakes should be at room temperature before you remove them from the pan.

10. Put a piece of parchment paper on a cookie sheet, sprinkle with sugar and, one at a time, turn the pans over and turn the cakes out onto parchment; the sugar will keep them from sticking. Refrigerate or freeze (page 284) until ready to decorate.

How to flour a cake pan:
To flour a cake pan, first grease with a thin, even layer of unsalted butter, nonstick spray, or vegetable oil, to coat it lightly. Add a small fistful of flour (about ¼ cup) to the center of the pan, tip the pan on its side, and rotate the pan to coat the inside with flour. Tap the pan gently on your work surface to loosen the excess flour, and return the excess to your flour container. Tap again and discard any lingering flour into the sink or garbage.

CHOCOLATE CAKE

{ MAKES TWO 9-INCH CAKES OR 24 CUPCAKES }

Along with vanilla, this is the safest choice for most cakes, but that doesn't mean it isn't delicious. For the best flavor and texture, be sure to use a high-quality cocoa.

1½ cups cake flour, plus more for
    flouring the cake pans
1½ cups granulated sugar, plus more
    for unmolding the cakes
½ cup (1 stick) unsalted butter, softened
    at room temperature
⅓ cup unsweetened Dutch-process
    cocoa powder
1 teaspoon baking soda
¼ teaspoon baking powder
⅓ cup melted unsweetened chocolate
    (such as Baker's), from two
    1-ounce squares
½ cup hot water
2 extra-large eggs
½ cup buttermilk
Unsalted butter (about 2 tablespoons)
    or vegetable oil, for greasing the cake
    pans (nonstick spray may also be used)

1. Position a rack in the center of the oven, and preheat to 350°F.

2. Put the flour, sugar, ½ cup butter, cocoa, baking soda, and baking powder in the bowl of a stand mixer fitted with the paddle attachment. (If you don't have a stand mixer, you can use a hand mixer, but take extra care not to overmix.) Mix on low speed just until the ingredients are blended, a few seconds, then raise the speed to low-medium and continue to mix until smooth, approximately 1 additional minute.

3. Stop the motor and pour in the chocolate. Mix for 1 minute on low speed. With the motor running, pour in the hot water. Add the eggs, one egg at a time, adding the next one after the previous one has been absorbed. With the motor still running, pour in the buttermilk. Stop the motor periodically and scrape from the bottom with a rubber spatula to be sure all the ingredients are fully integrated, and return the mixer to low-medium speed. Continue to mix for 1 additional minute to ensure the eggs are fully absorbed. This will also help ensure that all the sugar is dissolved and the flour is thoroughly mixed in, which will help produce a luxurious mouthfeel in the final cake. Before baking, be sure the batter is between 70° and

73°F, or the cake will crown. (If it is too warm, put it in the refrigerator for a few minutes; if too cool, let it rest at room temperature.)

4. Grease two 9-inch cake pans (2 inches deep) and flour them. (For more, see "How to Flour a Cake Pan," page 293.)

5. Divide the batter evenly between the two cake pans, using a rubber spatula to scrape down the bowl and get as much batter as possible out.

6. Bake until the cakes begin to pull from the sides of the pan and are springy to the touch, 25 to 30 minutes.

7. Remove from the oven and let cool for at least 30 minutes, preferably 1 hour. The cakes should be at room temperature before you remove them from the pan. Put a piece of parchment paper on a cookie sheet, sprinkle with sugar, and turn the cakes out onto parchment; the sugar will keep them from sticking. Refrigerate or freeze (page 284) until ready to decorate.

CARROT CAKE

{ MAKES TWO 9-INCH CAKES OR 24 CUPCAKES }

This is a straight-up classic carrot cake—dense and moist—with raisins and walnuts adding crunch and sweetness. It doesn't get along with a wide variety of frostings, but when paired with Cream Cheese Frosting (page 307) it's a form of perfection.

3 cups finely grated carrots (from about 5 large carrots)

2½ cups cake flour, plus more for flouring the cake pans

2 cups granulated sugar, plus more for unmolding the cakes

2 cups Italian Custard Cream (page 306), optional

¾ cup vegetable oil

2¼ teaspoons baking powder

2 teaspoons ground cinnamon

1 teaspoon baking soda

1 teaspoon pure vanilla extract

½ teaspoon fine sea salt

4 extra-large eggs

1 cup milk

½ cup chopped walnuts

¼ cup golden raisins

Approximately 2 tablespoons unsalted butter (about 2 tablespoons) or vegetable oil, for greasing the cake pans (nonstick spray may also be used)

1. Position a rack in the center of the oven, and preheat to 350°F.

2. Put the carrots, flour, sugar, custard (if using), oil, baking powder, cinnamon, baking soda, vanilla, and salt in the bowl of a stand mixer fitted with the paddle attachment. (If you don't have a stand mixer, you can use a hand mixer.) Mix on low just until the ingredients are well blended, a few seconds, then raise the speed to low-medium and continue to mix until the mixture is smooth, approximately 1 additional minute.

3. With the motor running, add one egg at a time, adding the next one after the previous one has been absorbed. Stop the motor periodically and scrape from the bottom of the bowl with a rubber spatula to incorporate. Return the mixer to low-medium speed.

4. Continue to mix for 1 additional minute to ensure that the eggs are fully absorbed. This will also help ensure that all the sugar is dissolved and the flour is incorporated, which will help produce a luxurious mouthfeel in the final cake.

5. With the motor running, pour in the milk, ½ cup at a time, stopping the motor to scrape the sides and bottom of the bowl between the two additions. Continue to mix for another 1 minute or until the mixture appears smooth. Add the walnuts and raisins and mix just to integrate them.

6. Grease two 9-inch cake pans with the butter, and flour them. (For more, see "How to Flour a Cake Pan," page 293.)

7. Divide the batter evenly between the two cake pans, using a rubber spatula to scrape down the bowl and get as much batter as possible out. Before baking, be sure the batter is between 70° and 73°F, or the cakes will crown. (Test by plunging a kitchen thermometer into the center of the batter; if it is too warm, put the bowl in the refrigerator for a few minutes; if too cool, let it rest at room temperature.)

8. Bake until the cake begins to pull from the sides of the pan and is springy to the touch, 25 to 30 minutes.

9. Remove from the oven and let cool for at least 30 minutes, preferably 1 hour. The cake should be at room temperature before you remove it from the pan.

10. Put a piece of parchment paper on a cookie sheet, sprinkle with sugar, and, one at a time, turn the pans over and turn the cakes out onto the parchment; the sugar will keep them from sticking. Refrigerate or freeze (page 284) until ready to decorate.

Note: *Carrots have a lot of moisture, so squeeze out their excess liquid by grating them, then putting them in a colander and pressing on them with a paper towel to keep the batter from being too wet or loose.*

RED VELVET CAKE

{ MAKES TWO 9-INCH CAKES, OR 24 CUPCAKES }

This is a classic in the American South that I fell in love with when it became nationally popular during the past decade or two. As with the Carrot Cake on page 296, this is best with Cream Cheese Frosting (page 307).

1¼ cups vegetable shortening

2 cups granulated sugar, plus more for sprinkling the parchment paper

1 tablespoon unsweetened Dutch-process cocoa powder

4½ teaspoons (2 tubes) red food-coloring gel

3 cups cake flour, plus more for flouring the cake pans

1¼ teaspoons fine sea salt

1¼ teaspoons pure vanilla extract

1¼ teaspoons baking soda

1¼ teaspoons distilled white vinegar

3 extra-large eggs

1¼ cups buttermilk

Unsalted butter (about 2 tablespoons) or vegetable oil, for greasing the cake pans (nonstick spray may also be used)

1. Position a rack in the center of the oven, and preheat to 350°F.

2. Put the shortening, sugar, cocoa, food coloring, flour, salt, vanilla, baking soda, and vinegar in the bowl of a stand mixer fitted with the paddle attachment. (You can use a hand mixer if you allow the shortening to soften at room temperature before beginning.) Paddle, starting at low speed, then raise the speed to low-medium and mix for about 1 minute. Add the eggs, one at a time, mixing for 1 minute after each is absorbed into the mixture. Add the buttermilk in two portions, stopping to scrape the sides of the bowl between additions.

3. Grease two 9-inch cake pans (2 inches deep) with the butter, and flour them. (See "How to Flour a Cake Pan," page 293).

4. Divide the batter evenly between the two cake pans, using a rubber spatula to scrape down the bowl and get as much batter as possible out.

5. Bake until the cakes begin to pull from the sides of the pans and are springy to the touch, 35 to 40 minutes.

6. Remove from the oven and let cool for at least 30 minutes, preferably 1 hour. The cakes should be at room temperature before you remove them from the pan.

7. Put a piece of parchment paper on a cookie sheet, sprinkle with sugar, and one at a time, turn the pans over and turn the cakes out onto the parchment; the sugar will keep them from sticking. Refrigerate or freeze (page 284) until ready to decorate.

FROSTINGS & FILLINGS

The following recipes produce the most popular cake frostings and fillings from Carlo's Bake Shop. They may become your go-to recipes for all your baking needs. Nothing would make me happier.

DECORATOR'S BUTTERCREAM

{ MAKES ABOUT 6 CUPS }

My recipe for Decorator's Buttercream, which you can adapt to make different colors. For white decorator's buttercream, or to dirty-ice a cake (Carlo's speak for applying a crumb coat, page 287) before applying fondant, you do not need to add any color.

This recipe can be multiplied or divided to produce larger or smaller batches, and leftover buttercream can be refrigerated right in a pastry bag or piped into another container and refrigerated for up to 2 weeks.

If you'd rather not make your own, you can also purchase Cake Boss frosting in place of Decorator's Buttercream.

7½ cups confectioners' sugar
2¼ cups vegetable shortening
¾ stick unsalted butter
1½ tablespoons pure vanilla extract
¼ cup plus 2 tablespoons cold water

1. Put the sugar, shortening, butter, and vanilla in the bowl of a stand mixer fitted with the paddle attachment and paddle at low-medium speed until the mixture is smooth, with no lumps, about 3 minutes.

2. With the motor running, add the water in a thin stream and continue to paddle until absorbed, about 3 minutes. The buttercream can be refrigerated in an airtight container for up to 2 weeks.

How Much Decorator's Buttercream?

There are amounts indicated for buttercream in the ingredients sections of the recipes in this book, but it's okay if you use a bit more or less than is indicated. As a rule of thumb, dirty-icing a cake will take about 4 cups of buttercream, leaving you 2 cups to use (and color as needed) for other purposes such as piping design elements or "gluing" fondant pieces to the cake. Dirty-ice the cake before coloring the remaining decorator's buttercream because you can return the icing you scrape off the cake while icing it to the bowl with the other uncolored buttercream, which will give you more to work with.

Making Different Colored Buttercreams

To color the cream, mix food coloring in with a rubber spatula until the cream is uniformly colored. Amounts will vary and will be based on the brand of food coloring and how light or dark you want the cream to be. I recommend food-coloring gel, available in small tubes, because it's less watery and easier to work with. Start with a small amount, and add more as you mix. If you are making a dark color, like black, the cream can become loose or watery in which case you should mix in some extra powdered sugar until the texture resembles shaving cream.

VANILLA FROSTING

{ MAKES ABOUT 4 CUPS, ENOUGH TO FILL AND ICE ONE 9-INCH CAKE }

For a creamier frosting, use milk instead of water. You must refrigerate this frosting, as well as any cakes filled or iced with it. Let it come to room temperature before using, and whisk briefly by hand to refresh it.

5 sticks unsalted butter, softened
5 cups powdered confectioners' sugar
1 tablespoon pure vanilla extract
¼ teaspoon fine sea salt
3 tablespoons lukewarm water

1. Put the butter in the bowl of a stand mixer fitted with the paddle attachment and mix on low speed until the butter is smooth with no lumps. With the motor running, add the sugar, 1 cup at a time, adding the next cup only after the previous addition has been integrated into the mixture.

2. Stop the machine and add the vanilla and salt. Paddle on low-medium speed until completely smooth, approximately 2 minutes. Add the water and continue to mix until light and fluffy, 2 to 3 minutes.

CHOCOLATE FUDGE FROSTING

{ MAKES ABOUT 4 CUPS, ENOUGH TO FILL AND ICE ONE 9-INCH CAKE }

For a creamier frosting, use milk instead of water. You must refrigerate this frosting, as well as any cakes filled or iced with it. Let it come to room temperature before using, and whisk briefly by hand to refresh it.

2½ cups (5 sticks) unsalted butter, softened

5 cups confectioners' sugar

⅔ cup unsweetened Dutch-process cocoa powder

1 tablespoon pure vanilla extract

¼ teaspoon fine sea salt

3 tablespoons lukewarm water

1. Put the butter in the bowl of a stand mixer fitted with the paddle attachment and paddle on low speed until smooth, with no lumps, approximately 3 minutes. With the motor running, add the sugar, one cup at a time, adding the next cup only after the previous addition is absorbed.

2. Stop the machine and add the cocoa, vanilla, and salt. Paddle on low-medium speed until completely smooth, approximately 2 minutes. Add the water and continue to paddle until light and fluffy, 2 to 3 minutes.

ITALIAN BUTTERCREAM

{ MAKES ABOUT 7 CUPS }

I adapted this recipe from one used at The Culinary Institute of America, shown to me by a group of students for whom I did a demonstration.

8 extra-large egg whites
2 cups granulated sugar
½ cup water
8 sticks unsalted butter, at room temperature, cut into small cubes

1. Put the whites in the bowl of a stand mixer fitted with the whip attachment.

2. Put 1½ cups of the sugar and the water in a heavy saucepan and bring to a boil over medium-high heat, stirring with a wooden spoon to dissolve the sugar. Continue to cook, without stirring, and bring to the soft ball stage (240°F).

3. Meanwhile, whip the whites at high speed until soft peaks form, approximately 5 minutes. With the motor running, add the remaining ½ cup sugar gradually, continuing to whip until medium peaks form.

4. When the sugar reaches 240°F, with the motor running, pour it into the egg whites, very slowly, in a thin stream, to avoid cooking the eggs. Raise the speed to high, and continue to whip until the mixture has cooled to room temperature, 10 to 15 minutes.

5. Stopping the motor between additions, add the butter in 5 increments, scraping the bowl with a rubber spatula before adding each addition of butter. With the motor running, add the vanilla, and whip just until it is blended in. The buttercream can be refrigerated in an airtight container for up to 1 week. Let it come to room temperature and paddle briefly before using.

ITALIAN CUSTARD CREAM

{ MAKES ABOUT 3 CUPS, ENOUGH TO FILL AND ICE ONE 9-INCH CAKE }

The longer you cook this cream, the thicker it will become, so you can—and should—adjust the texture to suit your taste.

2½ cups whole milk

1 tablespoon pure vanilla extract

1 cup granulated sugar

⅔ cup cake flour, sifted

5 extra-large egg yolks

2 teaspoons salted butter

1. Put the milk and vanilla in a saucepan and bring to a simmer over medium heat.

2. In a bowl, whip together the sugar, flour, and egg yolks with a hand mixer. Ladle a cup of the milk-vanilla mixture into the bowl and beat to temper the yolks.

3. Add the yolk mixture to the pot and beat over medium heat with the hand mixer until thick and creamy, about 1 minute. As you are beating, move the pot on and off the flame so that you don't scramble the eggs.

4. Remove the pot from the heat, add the butter, and whip for 2 minutes to thicken the cream. Transfer to a bowl. Let cool, cover with plastic wrap, and refrigerate at least 6 hours. Will keep for up to 1 week. To make chocolate custard cream, add 1½ ounces melted, cooled unsweetened chocolate along with the butter. For a richer chocolate flavor, add a little more.

CREAM CHEESE FROSTING

{ MAKES ABOUT 3 CUPS, ENOUGH TO FILL AND ICE ONE 9-INCH CAKE }

This is the classic filling and topping for two super-popular cakes: Carrot Cake (page 296) and Red Velvet Cake (page 298). I always make it with Philadelphia brand cream cheese, which I think is simply the best.

Two 8-ounce packages cream cheese
1 stick unsalted butter, softened
1 teaspoon pure vanilla extract
2 cups confectioners' sugar, sifted

1. Put the cream cheese and butter in the bowl of a stand mixer fitted with the paddle attachment and paddle at medium speed until creamy, approximately 30 seconds.

2. With the motor running, pour in the vanilla and paddle for 30 seconds. Add the sugar, a little at a time, and mix until smooth, approximately 1 minute after the last addition. Use this as soon as you make it, because it will get very stiff in the refrigerator. If you have to refrigerate it (for a maximum of 2 days), do not microwave it to freshen it. Instead, let it rest at room temperature for 4 hours to soften.

MY DAD'S CHOCOLATE MOUSSE

{ MAKES ABOUT 3½ CUPS, ENOUGH TO FILL AND ICE ONE 9-INCH CAKE}

We still make our chocolate whipped cream with my Dad's recipe. It's rich and fluffy and can be used on many different types of cake.

2 cups heavy cream
½ cup granulated sugar
3 tablespoons unsweetened Dutch-process
　　cocoa powder
1 tablespoon Kahlúa or other coffee liqueur

1. Put the cream, sugar, cocoa powder, and Kahlúa in a stainless-steel mixing bowl. Blend with a hand mixer at high speed until fluffy, about 1 minute.

2. Use immediately or refrigerate in an airtight container for up to 3 days.

CHOCOLATE GANACHE

{ MAKES ABOUT 2 CUPS }

This ganache can be used as a filling and/or poured over a cake. To use it as a filling, refrigerate it, transfer it to a pastry bag, and pipe it out following the directions on page 283.

To pour ganache over a cake, melt it in a double boiler and simply pour it over a cake or layer. To top layers of French cream or chocolate mousse with ganache, pour it on and smooth it with a cake icing spatula.

1 cup heavy cream
9 ounces semisweet chocolate, coarsely
   chopped
1 tablespoon light corn syrup

1. Put the heavy cream in a saucepan and set it over medium-high heat. As soon as it begins to simmer, remove the pot from the heat. Add the chocolate and stir with a wooden spoon to melt the chocolate. Stir in the corn syrup.

2. To cover a cake with poured ganache, set a wire rack in or over a baking tray. Set the cake on the rack. Carefully ladle the molten ganache over the cake in a steady stream, letting it run over the cake until uniformly covered.

   Otherwise, transfer to a bowl and refrigerate for about 1 hour. If using for filling, soften in a double boiler over medium heat until pourable.

3. Let any unused ganache cool, transfer to an airtight container, and refrigerate for up to 3 days. Reheat gently in a double boiler set over simmering water, stirring with a rubber spatula until warm and pourable.

LOBSTER TAIL CREAM

{ MAKES 5½ CUPS }

We use this decadent cream to fill our signature lobster tail pastries, and it can also be used to fill and/or frost cakes; it's especially delicious on our Vanilla Cake (page 292).

Italian Custard Cream (page 292)
Italian Whipped Cream (page 311)
2 tablespoons Baileys Irish Cream,
    plus more to taste, optional

1. Put the custard cream in a mixing bowl. Add the whipped cream, a little at a time, folding it in with a rubber spatula.

2. Drizzle the Baileys Irish Cream, if using, over the mixture, gently mixing it in. Add more to taste, if desired, but do not overmix the cream.

   The cream can be refrigerated in an airtight container for up to 4 days. Whisk briefly by hand to refresh before using.

ITALIAN WHIPPED CREAM

{ MAKES ABOUT 2½ CUPS }

This sweetened whipped cream can be used to fill and/or ice cakes, and is also a component of French cream and the cream we use to fill Carlo's famous lobster tails.

1½ cups heavy cream
¼ cup plus 2 tablespoons granulated sugar

1. Put the cream and sugar in a bowl and whip on high speed with a hand mixer. Do not overmix or you'll end up with butter.

2. The cream can be refrigerated in an airtight container for up to 3 days. Whisk by hand to refresh before using.

INDEX

ACKNOWLEDGMENTS

Wow, a fourth book! I never could have imagined we'd keep doing this once a year, and it's been an incredibly fun and rewarding experience. Much of that has to do with the invaluable participation of some key friends and family. My great thanks to the following people:

My immediate family: My wife, Lisa. My four incredible kids: Sofia, Buddy, Marco, and Carlo. My mother, Mary Valastro. And, now and forever, the memory of my father, Buddy Valastro, the original Cake Boss.

My four sisters: Grace, Madeline, Mary, and Lisa, and my brothers-in-law: Mauro, Joey, and Joe.

The crew at the bakery, especially Frankie, Danny, Leo, and Nikki.

Adam Bourcier and Vincent Tubito who manage the company's growth with calm and class.

My assistant, Victoria Auresto.

Andrew Friedman, for helping me get my thoughts on the page one more time.

Stacy Adimando, who tested the delicious recipes for this book.

Liz White, for her help with the cakes and other "showpiece" desserts for the photo shoots.

Photographer John Kernick for the beautiful photography, and to John's team: Digital tech Rizwan Alvi, grip Darrell Taunt, food stylist Adrienne Anderson, food stylist assistant Micah Morton, prop stylist Paige Hicks, and prop assistants Jenna Tedesco and Eddie Barerra.

The team at my publisher, Atria: President and Publisher Judith Curr, Associate Publisher Benjamin Lee, Senior Editor Leslie Meredith, Associate Editor Donna Loffredo, Senior Jacket Art Director Jeanne Lee, Assistant Director of Publicity Lisa Sciambra, Publishing Manager Jackie Jou, Senior Production Manager Jim Thiel, and Art Director Dana Sloan, as well as the team at 3&Co.: Amy Harte and Merideth Harte for their art direction and design of this book.

Jon Rosen and the team at William Morris Endeavor Entertainment, especially literary agent Eric Lupfer.

My extended family—my aunts and uncles, cousins and second cousins—and to all my friends. It's been great having you all along for such a fun ride, in front of the camera, and behind it.

My creative family at TLC and Discovery.

God, for his continued blessings to me and my family.

And, as always, to the customers of Carlo's Bake Shop, and to the fans of my show—you guys make it all possible, and I love you all.

ABOUT THE AUTHOR

Buddy Valastro is the star of the hit TLC series *Cake Boss*, *Next Great Baker*, and *Bakery Boss*, and author of the *New York Times* bestsellers *Cake Boss* and *Baking with the Cake Boss*, as well as *Cooking Italian with the Cake Boss*. He is owner and operator of Carlo's Bakery in Hoboken, New Jersey, with multiple Carlo's Bake Shops in the surrounding area. In addition, Buddy operates the Cake Boss Cafe in Times Square, New York City. Buddy lives with his wife and four children in New Jersey.